CRAFTING POETRY

OTHER PUBLICATIONS

The Craft of Writing Poetry
A Practical Poetry Course
How to Write 5-Minute Features
The Art of Writing Poetry
    (correspondence course)
How to Write About Yourself
    (with Brenda Courtie)
Writing Competitions: The Way to Win
    (with Iain Pattison)
The Handy Little Book of Tips for Poets
The Poet's Workbook
A Practical Guide to Poetry Forms

POETRY COLLECTIONS

Alone No More
    (with Robin Gregory)
Flying Free
Single Return
The Need for Unicorns
Paper Birds
Light Angles
Daring the Slipstream
Mapping the Maze
Hold Tight
Iced
Star and Snowflake

CRAFTING POETRY

A practical guide for anyone
wishing to learn or enhance the skills
of writing, refining, publishing and reading poetry

ALISON CHISHOLM

First published in 2010
by Caleta Publishing

ISBN   978-1-4457-7903-4

Printed and bound by Lulu.com

Alison wishes to acknowledge grateful thanks to all at Allison and Busby for their kindness and generosity, to Brenda for advice, and to Malcolm for hand-holding (both physical and metaphorical), meal-providing and proof-checking. So blame him if you find any typos.

CONTENTS

CHAPTER ONE

WHO WRITES?

If you go into a room full of people and ask all the poets to raise their hand, you will find very few responding. Then ask for anyone who has ever written a poem (other than as part of an English lesson in school) to raise their hand, and there will be a definite response. Many of those people will have written rather more than the single poem suggested. So what does it take to shift people from placing themselves in the second category to acknowledging the first? Courage? Artistry? Confidence? Insanity?

Most of us have the aptitude to write poetry in some shape or form. Not so many can write poetry well; but the good news is that almost everyone with some scrap of ability can build on it to improve their poems. The fact that you are sufficiently interested to be reading this book means that you have the potential to write good poetry. Try this simple quiz to gauge your aptitude.

1 Somebody gives you a poetry book for your birthday. Do you:
a give them a hug and say it's just what you wanted?

b thank them politely and check whether they've written in it? (You can always recycle by giving it to someone else.)
c find it impossible to stop yourself from blurting out 'But I wanted a book about POTTERY'?

2 You are happily reading the daily newspaper and you come across the new Poetry Column. Do you:
a read it? It's always good to find a new poem.
b turn the page? You're reading the paper for the news it contains.
c rip the page out to line the budgie's cage?

3 You are listening to the radio and the announcer says that the next programme will feature poems requested by listeners. Do you:
a sit down with a cuppa and enjoy the programme?
b get on with the jobs but listen with half an ear?
c turn the set off and start your letter of complaint to the station manager?

4 A friend rings and asks if she can pop round. She's just joined a creative writing class, and she wants to read you her poem. Do you:
a tell her to come and open a bottle of wine?
b tell her to come, but get a couple of glasses into your system before she arrives?
c tell her sorry, you're just waiting for the taxi to take you to the airport. Patagonia. For three months.

5 Your Granny sends you a Christmas card with a lovely verse by Patience Strong on the outside. Do you:
a read it and think Granny's sweet?
b glance at it then put it on display with your other cards?
c hide it deep in a drawer in case any of your friends should see?

You get the message. Don't bother totting up your a, b, c scores. But before you leave this daft little quiz, think for a moment. Did you read every question and each possible answer? Did you actually try to work out what you would do? Did you think of any other answers you might have given? If you can say yes to any of these, you've won the coconut. You have indicated a meticulous attention to detail, even when it seems trivial. You have sought out the individual and particular answer just as, when producing a poem, you would seek out the exact word or image that fits your meaning perfectly.

Now let's think back to all the people in that room. The ones who admitted to writing a poem on an odd occasion - but would not call themselves poets - are responding to an inner urge to make sense of something in their life, to try to understand some great truth, to acknowledge a specialness, to mark an occasion just as they could have done by taking a photo.

A poem has more dimensions than a photo. It has layers and can spark a profound emotional reaction. Or it can evoke a memory with a special richness born of its use of imagery. Or it can be written to be delivered on a joyous occasion, to add to the fun for the assembled company. Or it can offer a light little soundbite. Or it can explain the meaning of life. Tall order?

Remember that a poem is a versatile device. It is the essence of communication between two minds, between two people who may never meet. It's a way of letting someone else see through your eyes, or of baring your soul in tangible form. It is also a perfect excuse for sitting around doing nothing for a few hours. When anybody asks why you haven't put up that shelf or hoovered the hall, you can just tell them 'I'm working on my Art.' That shuts them up.

Going back to the people who write poetry ... you will have realised that there is no such thing as a typical poet; there are just people who respond to the world around them - and the universe within them - by writing poems.

Poets come from all walks of life and educational backgrounds. You don't need a degree to write a poem, but a little experience of life's knocks can be helpful. Poets come from every culture in the world, every creed and colour, both sexes. They may be of any age, working or not, loners or party animals, hunky or frumpy, rich or penniless, healthy or ailing. They may be driven to see their writing in print, or interested only in setting poems down for their own satisfaction, without thought of publication.

There will be some common ground. Poets tend to be interesting people, as they all have something to communicate. They love words. They like puns, anagrams, double meanings, cryptic crosswords, and have a sheer fascination with the way words work. They are keen observers, and they absorb and digest their observations, seeing patterns, meanings, logic and fantasy in them. They are without doubt the elite.

INSPIRATION V. PERSPIRATION

Can you imagine it? You are drifting through a wood enveloped in a velvet cloak, and preferably with a lily in your hand. Inspiration strikes. You find a convenient treetrunk and sit there for ten minutes while a perfect poem pours from your gold fountain pen onto the page of handmade paper you just happened to have about your person. You read the finished product aloud, and revel in the exquisite words you have produced. Squirrels and rabbits cluster at your feet, and bluebirds flirt the air about your head.

OK, we can dream. That is about as close to reality as a tin of spam is to fillet steak. But there needs to be a touch of the dreaming, a frisson of excitement that spurs you on.

A poem can come to you from a flash source, and when it does you can do nothing more than be thankful and murmur gratitude to your Muse, your God, your Inspiration ... however you see it. More often it starts as a few words, a snatch of thought, a phrase that insinuates itself into your mind, something you see, hear, smell, taste or touch that clings to your memory. Then other thoughts begin to flesh it out, pull it in different directions, and start you on the process of building up the poem.

It's a good idea to get these thoughts down as soon as you have them, so if you don't want your entire poetry output to be scribbled on the backs of gas bills and till receipts, get into the habit of carrying a notebook or electronic equivalent around with you at all times. Doing so ensures you will not have a chance to forget your brilliant idea before you can find somewhere to put it.

If you should lose this idea, it will assume a greater importance in your life than it deserves. You will feel bereft, as if the poem you were born to write can no longer be written. Much of this has to do with your frustration at not being able to recall the idea, of course, but that does not mean you feel its loss any the less.

If inspiration is the starting point for your poem, perspiration is the factor that brings your idea to fruition. Writing a quality poem is hard work. You can toss a few rhymes into the air without any effort, but you are unlikely to find personal or audience satisfaction with the result. The most satisfying poems are those into which you have poured something of yourself.

Even when you have only written a first draft, you should feel physically, mentally and emotionally exhausted, as if you were just recovering from a dose of 'flu. Further drafts will also drain you, but not quite as much. The first draft requires all your creative energy. The demands of re-drafting are onerous, but not quite so enervating.

When you feel you have produced a draft with which you are happy, there is still more hard work required. For now you have come to the redrafting and revision processes, where every part of the poem must be scrutinised to check that it is working on a communicative, technical, grammatical and artistic level.

More of this later. Any piece you write could become part of the world's stock of this incredible 'product', poetry. It could be around for centuries. It is worth taking pains to get it right.

WHO ARE YOU WRITING FOR?

- Yourself.
- Everyone else.

One of the greatest joys of writing poetry is the sense of pleasure and achievement you get when you have written it. You have taken a strand of thought and created a work of art from it. You have encapsulated your message, your dreams, your hopes, your wisdom in words. It doesn't matter whether your poem is profound or a tiny snapshot cameo.

The feeling is intensified when you can share it with other people. Look at the rapt faces in the audience when you are giving a reading, or the concentration in the writers' group when you are seeking feedback, and you will gain immense satisfaction. Now imagine thousands ... or let's be honest, more likely hundreds ... of readers who see your work on the page when it's published in a book or magazine. The chances are you will never meet them; but their thinking - their lives could be changed by what you have written. Yes, honestly.

WHAT ARE YOU WRITING FOR?

- Large sums of money.
- Pop legend/football star fame.

If you are expecting either of these - forget it. The majority of poets will never gain this sort of practical return for their writing.

If you adjusted the expectation to tiny sums of pocket money and a quick mention in your local paper, that would be a bit more realistic. If you expect nothing, you will be thrilled by the occasional small cheque or moment of recognition, but not disappointed if they never happen.

PREPARATION

Please read this section even if you are a published poet who writes regularly. We're going to look at the preparation you need to put in place simply to be a poet, but this preparation needs to be 'topped up' frequently. Think of it like going on a diet. You can lose a lot of weight all at once, but if you don't change to a healthier way of eating, you will pile the pounds on again. You can get yourself into the mindset of a poet, but if you don't stay in that frame of mind, your poetic dynamism will wane.

This five-point plan will help you to get into peak condition for writing poetry; and if you repeat it every week or every month, will help you to stay there.

1 Read poetry. Read voraciously from all periods, enjoying the poetry of the past for the sheer pleasure of it, and relishing the poetry of today as the backdrop against which your own writing will appear.

2 Take a poem and deconstruct it, studying it analytically. Ask yourself what its author was thinking about during the writing process. What is its essential message, and is it communicated effectively? How has the writer used language, form, grammar, metaphor, imagery, etc. to flesh out the message? Consider all these points not from the angle of a literary critic, but from the standpoint of a fellow poet.

3 Play with poetry in your head. Memorise passages you love. Think up clever rhymes. Make up limericks about your friends - or better, about your enemies. Work out riddles and anagrams. Have fun with language.

4 Write an entry in your notebook or journal. This should not be a poem, but should demonstrate your affinity with language, your observations and responses. It may include ideas for poems you plan to write in the future. (Notebooking is considered more fully in the next chapter).

5 Write the first draft of a poem. Don't worry if it isn't perfect, but do try to get a whole idea down on paper in initial draft format. You will never recapture the exact circumstance of writing if you have to leave a first draft and come back to it later. Look at Coleridge. If it had not been for the interruption of that dratted 'person on business from Porlock', *Kubla Khan* might have been as long and as gripping as *The Ancient Mariner*.

At this stage, I know that some people will be muttering that this is a preposterous formula, that it won't work, and that you didn't invest time and energy in reading a book only to be given all these impertinent instructions. That's a valid argument. Just as there is no such thing as a typical poet, there is no such thing as a magic formula to enhance someone's skills as a poet. But before you dismiss the five-point plan, give it a fair trial. Then tweak the bits you like least and add some techniques of your own. If you try doing this for a while and still feel there is no benefit, stop doing it.

You can apply this get-out clause to anything you read here, or in any book about the craft of writing poetry. At the end of the day, your poem is yours, and you must be totally happy with it. All the hints and words of advice offered work for a lot of poets, but they won't work for everyone.

EXERCISES

At the end of each chapter, you will find five exercises to tone up your 'writing muscle', trigger a new poem, or generally assist you in your writing life. Here, too, it is appropriate to try them out, either as you complete the study of the chapter or during your available writing time over the next few days. Again, you may find that not everything works for you; but you cannot be sure until you have tried. Wherever possible, the exercises have been designed in an open fashion, so that you can return to the same instructions repeatedly and find a new stimulus each time.

Some people argue that poems triggered by exercises can never be as good as the ones that reach you 'naturally', through inspired ideas or observations. This does not have to be the case. Whenever you are writing a poem, there is the potential for you to reach the take-your-breath-away moment, when you realise something stunning is happening on the page. It can happen whether the idea came from an exercise or in some epiphanal flash of revelation.

You can't pre-empt or force the moment, and it doesn't always happen; but when it does you know that your writing has transcended the pedestrian and become something very special. You will have your own individual way of recognising it. (I call it the third glass of champagne effect, because my lips go numb and my knees start to wobble.) The work you produce still needs to be subjected to rigorous revision, but it has a head start because it has attained the 'tingle factor.'

See if your work on any of these ideas starts the tingle.

1 Think of a momentous day in your childhood, such as the day you started school, or the day you had your tonsils out. Now recall it via each of the five senses. Write a couplet about each sense, leaving white space between them, so that you end up with five two-line stanzas. Don't try to enforce rhyme or metre; just write. If you wish, add a final couplet of reaction or emotional

response. The fact that you can only write two lines for each sense makes you selective and specific; there may be a lot to put across in a few words ... and of course that's what poetry is all about. Go back through the poem to see if you can tighten your writing, perhaps by cutting non-essential words or expressing a phrase more tautly, and to check whether you could substitute any words to produce sound similarities or greater precision.

2 Look at the view from your window. Fix on one detail of it - a cloud, a brick in the wall, a passer-by. Now apply the writer's best friend, the phrase *What if...?* Make a list of possibilities, from the logical to the ludicrous, then let your imagination take off. Just get words onto paper. You can mould your writing into a poem later if you wish.

3 This one needs a steady hand. Take a contemporary poetry magazine you've finished with, and cut out one of the poems, preferably an unrhymed one of no more than twenty lines. Make a photocopy of it, but try not to study it too carefully. Cut the poem into separate lines. (This is where the steady hand comes in). Now go away and do something entirely different for an hour or so. When you come back to the poem, arrange the lines into the order you think works. Compare the resulting poem with the original. Which is better? Why? Or are they identical? This is no mere game. It makes you focus on every word and its usage.

4 Recall a nursery rhyme. Now change the last line (or lines) to something absurd, funny, distressing, risqué or more up-to-date. This is just an idle moment's activity - but do it often enough and you might create a collection of new nursery rhymes.

5 Write a detailed description of the last time you were out in the snow, avoiding all the clichés and not mentioning the word *white*. What did you do? Did you enjoy the weather or not?

How were you affected by it? You can return to this exercise using rain without mentioning *wet*, sun without *hot* and similar.

CHAPTER TWO

HOARDING NOTES

For most poets, there are times when the ideas tumble together so quickly it's almost impossible to decide which to explore first. Then there are times when nothing seems to come, and you feel nothing ever will, even though the urge to be writing is constant. You can support the frenetic times and provide material for the fallow ones by hoarding information, ideas and sources.

It's useful to get into the habit of keeping both a notebook and a journal - an ideal situation for stationery junkies - and writing in them frequently; though not, perhaps, putting yourself under pressure to write every day. That can be counter productive. You only have to miss a few days, and you're either racing around hunting for extra input to compensate for the omission, or you decide it's not worth the trouble and give up.

Your notebook is for everything that strikes you as you go about your daily business. It could contain an interesting rhyme you've just thought of, a description of a flower you noticed in a hedge, a snippet of overheard conversation, (always a delicious source for poetry), notes to remind you of a half-forgotten memory that has just drifted into your mind. Be sure to record your emotions, feelings and reactions here too. Even if you never use them in a poem about the circumstance that prompted them, you will be able to transfer them into any different circumstances to bring integrity of reaction into poems on other themes. Carry your notebook around with you to be sure you never miss an opportunity to jot something down. Trawl it frequently, taking time to marvel at your notes.

The journal is a more formal document, and something you might set aside time for writing in, while being aware of the caveat mentioned above. The best journals are a jumble of thoughts, memories complete with your emotions and response to them, and half-formed ideas, dreams and feelings, extracts from newspapers and letters, quotations etc. The big difference is that they tend to be written more carefully and in greater depth than the notebook scribbles. Here, too, it is worth making regular checks to be surprised and thrilled by the contents.

NOTEBOOK TO DRAFT

When you light on a theme for your poem, either through an exercise or from a flash source, the initial toying with the idea happens inside your head. You play around with different thoughts, examining all facets of them to see what potential lies there. Then the idea needs to be transferred to - or back to - paper. No matter how clear your thought processes, you will find it difficult to develop a poem in construction until you start putting things down. Even when you are dealing with a 'donné', the gift of a poem that presents itself to you in a near-complete and working format, it's worth subjecting it to an early-development exercise, as all ideas can discover extra momentum when you allow yourself to play with them. Some poets have a favourite device for managing this first stage; but it's a good idea to let the poem decide how its genesis should take place. For just as every poet is an individual, so every poem has its own individuality.

Sometimes you find that the first written explorations of the budding poem are already appearing in the pattern of poetry, especially in the case of a donné. It may be that some form of lineation and/or division into stanzas, (verses), will fall naturally from the pen. You may even detect a pattern of rhyme and metre emerging in this initial phase. If this happens, let lines form themselves as they will. There is plenty of time to knock them into a better shape later. Don't engage in too much conscious thought. Allow yourself to be carried along by the momentum of the emerging poem.

If your first reactions to the subject are not so fleshed, start with a simple word-gathering exercise, using an association of ideas to produce your raw material. Write a key word at the top of your page, and then list all the thoughts that enter your head in response to it. Start a new line for each new thought, both to space your work (making it easier to read) and to give it the appearance of an aligned (and therefore poetic) pattern on the page.

Another useful approach is flow-writing. Again, you begin with a key word or phrase, but instead of going through logical thought processes, you just write. Write quickly, and try not to stop writing, even if your thoughts dry up and you find yourself repeating a word or phrase. Restrict the amount of time you spend on this to two or three minutes, and don't be tempted to read what you have written until the time is up.

At the end of your time allocation, look back through the writing, and highlight any words or phrases that strike you as interesting. They may be strictly related to the key word, or unexpected and apparently unconnected. There may already be an avenue into a poem revealing itself through the writing. If there is not, repeat the flow-writing exercise using one of the words/phrases you have highlighted as the trigger. You can continue doing this any number of times, until a route into the poem emerges.

An alternative to this is to create a flow chart of ideas, also known as a mind map or cluster. This is like the list of thoughts, but forms a different pattern on the paper, which can guide your thinking differently. Here you start with a key word or phrase in the centre of your page, surround it with a box, and then allow spokes to radiate from the box, placing each associated idea in its own secondary box at the end of a spoke. New trains of thought occupy new boxes, but further associations from one idea to the next can create satellites to the secondary boxes. Continue until you have created a web of spokes and boxes, which may be simple or extremely complex. Again, limit your time to force yourself to think dynamically.

To develop this exercise, simply look back at the web you have created, and trace the route which you think would be the most stimulating to explore in a poem. You do not have to restrict yourself to one path through the web. Experiment by cross-matching different threads, and you may spot all sorts of stimulating links from your initial material. You may find content for additional poems. If this is the case, try using differently coloured highlighter pens, marking associated thoughts for one poem in blue, another set in pink and so on.

Whichever path you follow at this point in the process, your ultimate intention is the same. You are aiming towards a first draft of a poem that will eventually communicate your idea into the mind of your reader.

WHILE YOU DRAFT ...

There are a few factors you need to keep in mind all the time you are producing the initial draft. Here are some general ones. Extend the list by adding in the factors that are especially important to you.

1 Your aim is to write something original. This is extremely difficult when people have been creating poems for thousands of years. It has all been said before. So why should a reader devote

time and attention to your version of an idea? Maybe because you give that reader:

- a new slant on a familiar theme, perhaps something that has never yet been considered. Countless poets have written about April showers, but how many of them have viewed the shower from the angle of a raindrop following the route from cloud to puddle, and its reactions on the way down?

- your unique way of looking at the world. Nobody has ever seen through your eyes before, so if you write with absolute fidelity to the truth as you see or interpret it, you have a good chance of producing something breathtakingly new.

- a link, joining your poem's subject with another idea/s, so that connections are made in two or more separate strands of thought. By exploring two different ideas, you can produce unexpected resonances. By focussing on both of these subjects within the same poem, you will have a statistically greater opportunity of coming up with ideas and angles the reader has never encountered.

Above all, you should never forget that a poem which merely rehashes old material has no real validity. If your poem is to be worth its paper, it should be giving the reader something new and fresh, something extra. A reader response of *I'd never thought of it like that* is highly desirable. The worst reader response is *So what?*

2   Poems are born out of a combination of experience and imagination. Sometimes the balance between these is level, and at others tipped heavily one way or the other. Experience can be broken down into personal memories, recollections of things you have been told about directly, and information you have gathered indirectly, via books and television for example. Imagination is anything you don't know, but that your mind can conceive;

anything from what's going on in your cat's head, to the description of a colour never known before, to the natural history of an invented planet on the other side of the universe. Keep reminding yourself of the scope of these elements, and of the infinite possibilities they create for you; and you will engage with the enormity of the task of writing the poem.

3 Be prepared to take pains for your poem. You may need to spend time and effort on research, with visits to other locations, art galleries, football grounds, museums, teashops etc. to absorb atmosphere, followed by hours studying books or trawling the net. Perhaps you need to explore new forms and approaches to find the perfect way into your writing. Maybe you need to rack your emotions, putting yourself through feelings and memories you would prefer to forget in order to find your poem's emotional truth. If you are dedicated to your idea, you will go to these lengths.

4 Remember that art and craft go together in a poem. The most brilliant idea will founder if it is poorly communicated. No matter how good that idea is, it will only become a good poem if its mechanics are honed and tuned to perfection.

5 Always remember the writers' maxim: *show, don't tell*. If you can make the reader feel involved in the action, become an organic part of the poem, you will have achieved.

6 While you are in the midst of a surge of creativity, your emerging poem may go spinning away along an unexpected track. There are three possible reasons for this:
- You have completely lost control. Draw the poem back to the route you had intended for it; but when you get to the revision stage, look very carefully at the point where the writing diverged from your plan for it. There may be a problem that needs attention.

- There is a better idea lurking in the poem. Sometimes you need to be engaged in the actual writing before a stronger idea presents itself. Be prepared to abandon your poem in order to follow a more thrilling path.
- There are two poems trying to be written. No problem. This is a bonus, like a BOGOF offer in a supermarket. Jot down the notes for the new idea as quickly as you can, without losing the thread of the initial idea. That's your next project.

7 It's always useful to write with your notebook to hand. While you are in the middle of producing a poem, your mind is perfectly geared up to poetry in general - or rather, it should be. So it isn't surprising that the most fertile time for coming up with new themes and subjects is when you are busy writing.

8 Never write with less than 100% devotion to the task. 105% is better.

PLANNING AHEAD

One of the problems for a poet is that every new day brings a new sheet of paper, insisting that you write another poem. This makes huge demands on your creative energy. You don't have the luxury of building new work onto yesterday's labours as you would if you were writing a novel or script. Yesterday's poem has already moved beyond the initial phase and into the 'redraft pending' part of the process. You are looking at a piece of blank paper. If you are lucky, an idea is burning in your mind, but you can't count on it. The more experienced you are as a poet, the more difficult it is to come up with the stunning new piece. You have said so much before, and you don't want to go over old ground again.

By doing some forward planning, you can keep a wealth of ideas bubbling up in preparation for treatment, and the blank page becomes an invitation rather than a threat. To achieve this, it's useful to spend some free time, possibly a whole writing session, coming up with a list of ideas you want to tackle.

You can include the harvest of notebook/journal material in this list, but also add memories you would like to explore more deeply, philosophical thoughts into which you can delve, reactions to items in the news, writing exercises you would like to try, fresh angles on familiar themes, narrative ideas, etc.

Doing this has two advantages. The first is that after the initial list-gathering, you do not have to spend precious writing time (and it is precious, as writers have busy lives) trawling your brains for a new idea to satisfy your urge to create. The second is that when you have thought of a list of themes to attack, even though you may not have been working on them consciously, your subconscious has been aware of them. When you return to them some time later, a little of the work has already been done. You recall them to mind, and there are already extra chunks of thought adhering to them; so instead of a simple trigger there is a complex knot of information and imagination clamouring for your attention.

EXERCISES

6 Go outside and find a small natural object, such as a leaf or stone. Examine it minutely. Write a detailed description of it using fresh and unexpected vocabulary. Does it have a scent or texture that interests you? What pleases you about it, what doesn't please you, and why? What associations arise in your mind when you look at it? What illogical thoughts flash into your mind at the same time? Now draft a poem, remembering to make it original and different from every other poem written about a natural object.

7 Take the same object you found for exercise 6 and ascribe to it some magical quality or power. Write a fantasy poem, for adult or child readers, exploring this.

8 Make a list of your favourite poems, then arrange them into a 'top ten'. Justify the placings.

9 Do you remember your dreams? Write a narrative poem describing the events of a dream or nightmare. You may find it helps to include repetition, perhaps a refrain of a few words or a complete line.

10 Think of a fairytale. Who is the key character, with whom the reader is meant to identify? For example, in Jack and the Beanstalk the reader is supposed to identify with Jack. Write a persona poem, in which you assume the viewpoint of a specific character other than the key character. The poem should tell the story from the angle of the other character, or put across that person's point of view. In the example mentioned, a persona poem could be told from the angle of Jack's mother, the giant, the man with the magic beans, or the cow who is exchanged for them. Respectively, the poems might express frustration with an annoying son; rage, grief and loss; a conman's jubilation turning sour as realisation of the beans' power dawns on him; or annoyance at being treated as a chattel instead of one of the family.

CHAPTER THREE

FINDING YOUR OWN VOICE

From an early stage in a poem's production, you may already be thinking about the voice through which it speaks. This presents something of a paradox. Each poem should have its own voice, perfectly suited to its contents. Yet poets, while striving to write fresh, original work and be true to every poem's individuality, want to develop a personal style which is immediately recognisable as their own. One of the most pleasing comments that can be made about your work is to have someone say *I read it, didn't know who had written it, guessed it was yours.*

Your own voice is born of your style. Unfortunately there is no short cut to its development. You cannot decide you are going to adopt a particular voice and then just do so. Your fingerprint on a poem will evolve through all the writing you undertake.

The best way to ensure that you are working towards an identifiable style is to keep writing. In common with other crafts, the more you write poetry the more easily you will be able to do it. And as your store of finished pieces increases, the idiosyncrasies of your writing which comprise your style will become better known to your readers, who will learn to identify your voice through them.

As we have considered, it's a tall order to identify an area of subject matter about which nobody has written before. Your style imprinted on the subject matter will bring a unique touch to it. The images you employ go a good way towards achieving this uniqueness.

IMAGERY

The message of your poem is clothed in a series of images to communicate it to the reader. The images are descriptions which appeal to the senses and to the emotions, conjuring up in the reader's mind perceptions of your writing that will bring it to life.

The best and strongest images are specific and concrete, not vague and waffly. William Carlos Williams talked of *no ideas but in things* - a good maxim for every poet to carry.

Through the imagery you use, you are projecting your persona, your own individuality, into your writing. We all see the world in a different way. Ask ten people to describe an event they have witnessed, and you will get ten different answers. That is because we each respond in a unique fashion, and filter the information that infiltrates our consciousness, retaining what is relevant for us, and discarding the rest. The bare bones of the event will be recalled by everyone, but the details will vary enormously. Ask any member of the police who has taken witness accounts of an event, and you will be told how great the variance can be.

When you write a poem, you are dealing in minutiae, the details that enable you to convey your message with exactness. You will weave a pattern of effects into your poem using the images that are significant for you. This is one of those factors that gives your poem its unique quality, speaking out with your individual voice.

As an example, let us look at one of the most hackneyed areas of writing poetry - a response to a disaster reported in the news. Imagine that a tanker has been damaged, and an oil slick appeared on the sea.

Everyone writing on the subject is aware of this basic fact. Some will know nothing more, but rely on imagination to supply further information. Others will have seen follow-up material in the papers and graphic pictures on the TV, checked out the internet, or heard radio descriptions of the event.

Whether or not they have gleaned additional information on the story, poets could pick up any of these ideas:

- The immediate ecological damage to the water/shoreline.
- The long-term ecological damage in the area.
- Condition of the seabirds.
- Death of fish.
- Damage to plankton and micro-organisms in the sea.
- Potential dangers for humans using the beach.
- The appearance of the slick as it moves.
- The effect of detergent used to disperse the oil.

The resulting poem is likely to touch on the basic facts of the disaster, but emphasise the details of one or more of these facets.

The facet highlighted and the way it is treated will depend on the writer's background and interests. Sometimes there are obvious clues to indicate which way the poet's mind is likely to go. If someone is a keen angler, an oil billionaire, a swimmer, ecologically aware, or a bird watcher, you can make assumptions about the direction of their thoughts. Respectively, the first image chosen to communicate a response might be:

- Fish twisting and lashing in agony.
- The bad press coverage for the oil industry.
- The risks of swimming in polluted waters.

- Harm inflicted by the tanker owner/captain on the environment.
- A seagull covered in oil.

Less easy to predict is the response from factors which are not publicly known. An irrational fear of birds, a childhood injury sustained at the seaside, shares in the shipping industry, or a liking for fish and chips will colour the manner of the response. A recurring nightmare about an octopus is the sort of wild card no one could ever expect.

So we can see how poets writing with total fidelity to their thoughts, convictions and experiences will produce a piece compatible with their own persona, and supplemented by their own imaginative processes.

For the circle of communication to be complete, the poem has to be picked up by a reader. At this point, another imponderable enters the equation.

Readers bring their own preferences, prejudices and imagination to their perception of the poem. Like the poet, they will have reactions based on their experiences, lifestyle, thoughts and dreams. Their reception of the poem is going to be influenced by these.

So just as every poet would feed something different into a poem on a given subject, every reader will digest something different from the piece. On a surface level, the reader may relate to or disagree with the information the poem communicates. On a deeper level, everyone who reads will be absorbing resonances from the poem which will be personally relevant.

This personal reaction to the poem is a guarantee of the singular quality of the piece of writing. No two people would write the same poem - no two people would read it in the same way.

Bring poet and reader together (intellectually rather than physically) and the poem springs into life with its own identity, and sings its message.

CHOOSING THE WORDS

In a poem, every word counts. Its meaning, resonances and the sound it makes when spoken all contribute to the final effect. The English language is rich in words, and within its vast vocabulary is everything you need to articulate your message with clarity. This makes it frustrating to read a poem whose writer has not thought around the vocabulary sufficiently to ensure that every word is exactly right. In a well written poem, it should be inconceivable to imagine any alternative to the words used.

This does not mean that a poem needs to be crammed with fancy language. Some of the most exciting poems are written in short, plain words. The excitement lies in their combinations and resonances. If you don't believe this, look up Robert Frost's *Stopping by Woods on a Snowy Evening*. The most exotic word in the entire poem is *downy*, and the longest is *promises*. And yet the magic of this piece echoes in the mind long after you have put the book aside.

One point should always be remembered: whether we like it or not, ours is a changing language. Words acquire new meanings, and a familiar word can be turned about. Whenever you use one of these fluid words, you can't get away from this fact. Every nuance of meaning, every atom of change is there in your vocabulary. Be aware of it. It's an enriching factor, not an impoverishment.

It might seem perverse to talk of the 'rules' of writing poetry, when the best poetry is the innovative sort that appears to have no rules. But there are some guidelines to word choice that may be applied to ensure your poem uses vocabulary to best effect. In general the following ten facets of vocabulary need to be treated with extreme caution.

1   Archaic words. The language of Tennyson, Keats and Wordsworth was perfect for the time when these masters of poetry were writing. It is no longer appropriate. *Thee* instead of

you, *yon* instead of *that*, and *ere* when you mean *before* will elicit groans from any discerning reader. *Morn* should never replace *morning*, even if it does rhyme conveniently - and horribly predictably - with *dawn*. Twee contractions are similarly unfortunate. When did you last hear anyone say *ne'er* for *never*, or *o'er* in place of *over*? They are obsolete in poetry just as they are obsolete in conversation.

2 Abstract words. These are a handy medium for expressing a broad thought without paying attention to its focus. Absence, melancholy, love and grief are familiar themes for poetry, but any of those words used within a poem is weak because it describes a broad concept. Analyse what the concept means to you, and then clothe it in words which convey that meaning. Don't be *sad*. Show *the knot that squeezes tears*. Don't be *ecstatic*. Describe *a fizz tingling thrills in the spine*.

3 Non-essential 'worker' words. When you write in prose, it is necessary to make frequent use of definite and indefinite articles, conjunctions etc., to make complete sense. In poetry these words may often be deleted. Their deletion has the effect of tightening the lines and heightening the effect you are creating. You can't, however, simply go through a poem and cross out every *the*. If you did, your poem would sound too clipped, a shorthand version of your message. But if you cut out every *the* and then reinstated only those that were essential to the flow of the writing, you would create a more vital poem. It's been suggested that the level of inexperience of a poet is commensurate with the number of times *the* appears.

4 Over-poetic words. A poem may be able to sustain a single unusual and overtly poetic word, but you are pushing your luck if you try to make it hold too many. *Anodyne* and *sylvan* can make the most soft-centred reader shudder. *Soul* is suspect, and *strand* (as in shore) needs to be treated with caution. The list is not constant. Watch out for any words that are becoming over-used

in a selfconsciously poetic fashion. Remember that every time you use one, you risk weakening your writing.

5 Repeated words. There are some set forms of poetry that rely on repetition for their structure. In a pantoum, for example, every line appears twice. Repetition is a legitimate device in a poem, and it can highlight a thought, creating a powerful effect. Try, however, to avoid unscheduled repetition, remembering how much attention is paid to the poem's every word. An unwarranted repeat will seem to the reader to be intentional, which alters the emphasis of meaning. If something that's *dark* at the start of the poem remains *dark* half way through, its darkness is compounded - fine if that was your intention, inappropriate if it was not. If you use *solid* in line six, avoid *solidity* in line seven. Refer to *mass, bulk, shape, weight* etc. instead.

6 Adverbs. In poetry, you can usually strengthen the image you are creating by deleting an adverb in favour of a more telling verb. Take the motion of the sea. If the tide comes in slowly, it would be more graphic to say it *creeps* or *crawls* in. Rather than coming in strongly, it could *crash* or *thunder.* Instead of coming in quickly, it could *surge.* Whenever you are tempted to include a qualifier for a verb, ask yourself whether there is a more precise verb you could have chosen instead.

7 Twee euphemisms. A poem that refers to a baby as an *angel* or a *cherub* is denying a truth. This truth may be sacrificed to the writer's sincerely held view, but there is a need to consider the sensibilities of the reader. I can give myself a fit of the vapours by contemplating writing a poem about cats, as I fear I could not resist the urge to mention *ickle-pretty-teeny-tiny-kittenkins.* And anything which makes the reader reach for the bucket is a bad idea. Similarly, the dead frog may have been trodden on, but it has not *passed over to a better place.* And in any poem, the heroine who faces *a fate worse than death* deserves all she gets.

8 Adjectives. These are not such literary lepers as adverbs, but should still be used with caution. An occasional adjective adds colour to your writing. Use too many, and your readers feel as though they are squelching through mud. Beware of using adjectives that add nothing to the sense of what you are saying. Night implies that the scene is *dark, late, velvet*, etc. One adjective specifies the kind of night you wish to conjure in the reader's mind; three obscure the picture.

9 Clichés. There are occasions in a poem when you can surmise exactly what will come next - because it has been used in that context many times before. If the moon shines in June, somebody is certain to *spoon* or to *swoon*. Hearts, minds and souls always seem to *ache*. And if anything breaks the silence, ten to one it's the sound of the lark. Clichés attain their status because they are accurate, but their predictability is dull in a poetic context. Surprise, and you will create a more memorable poem.

10 Words designed to shock. Some poets spatter their work with expletives in the same way that a small child learns to embarrass his Mum by shouting 'rude' words in a crowded bus. There are times when crude vocabulary is perfect to convey the message you are trying to put across; but usually a resort to scatological or obscene language is a device to disguise an inadequate vocabulary.

You may be thinking there are not many words left that can be used with impunity. Now that you have read the catalogue of anticipated problems, forget it while you allow all the words that come into your head to pour onto the paper and articulate the poem you are writing.

Don't forget to return to the catalogue, though, and check every word when the first excitement of producing the poem has passed. Wordsworth spoke of poetry as *emotion recollected in tranquillity.* Tranquillity is not just for reflecting on emotions, but for checking word use as well.

WORDPLAY

More than any other writers, poets have carte blanche to play about with the words they use. First it is worth thinking a little about the sounds those words create. The best poetry works equally well when read silently from the page and when recited aloud. In silent form, the words are only heard within the confines of the mind. When spoken, their full sound values may be appreciated.

While selecting the vocabulary for your poem, think about the use of onomatopoeia. This occurs when the words allow a speaker to infuse them with a sense of the feeling or action they are trying to communicate. Try saying words like *hiss*, *kick*, *mellifluous* and *buzzing* to demonstrate its effectiveness.

Now let's consider the way the pronunciation of language can alter the weight of a syllable.

There are three lengths of vowel sound - monophthongs, diphthongs and triphthongs. A monophthong, or single sound, requires just one impulse of voice to produce it. *A* as in *cat*, *o* as in *box* and *e* as in *fed* are examples of these. Their shortness lends itself to a staccato reading.

Diphthongs are formed when one sound elides into another to make a longer vowel, such as *air* where *e* and *u* are combined, or *ay*, where *e* joins with *ee*. The nature of these sounds indicates that they will take longer to pronounce, and therefore produce a marginally more drawn-out effect.

Triphthongs combine three sounds. In the word *fire*, the vowel consists of *a*, *i* and *u* spoken in rapid succession to produce the composite *-ire*. These take a fraction more time to pronounce than either of the other forms.

Although each of these types of vowel produces one syllable when spoken, the syllable length will be altered by the degree of movement that elision through the sounds requires. Taking the same consonant sounds, try using a monophthong, diphthong and triphthong, and see how much space each occupies, eg:

monophthong	*fed*
diphthong	*fade*
triphthong	*fired*

Remember that each of these is correctly pronounced as a single syllable.

Now consider the consonant sounds you are using as well. A plosive sound is shorter and sharper than a sustained sound. *T* and *b* are produced more briskly than *f* and *l*. A multiple of consonants extends the sound produced. Try saying *sing*, then *sting*, and then *string*. Each consonant/consonantal cluster is part of a single syllable, and yet they occupy different quantities of sound space.

When you consider vowel length in conjunction with consonant length, you realise just how much leeway there is within the sound space of one syllable. For example, each of the six words in this sentence consists of one syllable:

The cat hid in the bag.

Equally, each of the six words in this sentence consists of one syllable:

Shy Jane lies down, yawns, smiles.

It's easy to see how you can change the feel, pace and mood of your poem by careful attention to the sounds of the words you are writing.

As well as studying sounds within the word, it is good practice to examine the way in which you use language. Poetry allows us the most innovative use of words. It is not always necessary to follow an expected grammatical pattern, for example. A noun can be converted into a verb, as in:

they coffeed until dawn
or
I vase the flowers.

It is not too great a leap of the imagination to assume that these phrases mean *they drank coffee until dawn* and *I put the flowers in the vase.* These prosaic expressions have been brought to life by the unexpected word usage. Of course, this doesn't always work; you may look at the examples above, think of a dozen more, and decide they are all plain silly. But whether they eventually appear in a poem or not, playing with them has allowed you a valuable moment practising word manipulation.

The technique is not limited to nouns and verbs. Mix and match various elements of grammar, experiment, and discover a unique writing style as you do so.

You can extend this experimentation into phrases by seeking out original similes and - more imaginatively - metaphors. Everyone has heard about being *as dead as a doornail,* but to be *as dead as a coin,* *a hand* or *a wallaby* is unusual. If you can find a logical association to make the simile work, you will have an original example to include in a poem. The conversion into a metaphor would create a person who was *coin-dead,* or *three hands dead,* or *in dead wallaby land.* This will only work for a reader if the simile or metaphor is clear and comprehensible. The three examples given above are absolute nonsense – unless, say, the first is part of a poem that uses a sustained metaphor linking the idea of money with the concept of old age and death.

Creating your own words is fascinating. Remember that their meaning must be comprehensible to all your readers. Your new words cannot be checked in the dictionary. A reader could probably surmise that a *shoulderall* is a large rucksack; but if you called it a *chitherparticiser* you would flummox the nation. If no word exists to convey your meaning precisely, making up a new one is an intriguing pastime. Look at J. K. Rowling's *Harry Potter* novels to see masterly handling of this practice. Don't be tempted to scatter new words merely as an affectation. Use them because they are a perfect device for your poem.

In fact, any unexpected device within your writing can be exciting and effective. But as soon as you begin to use it merely to show evidence of your great skill with language, the object of the exercise is lost, and you run the risk of disappearing up the obscurity of your own cleverness.

THE BORING BIT

Few of us are enthused by the elements of grammar and punctuation; but if your poem is to be truly effective, it's worth concentrating on them. If both are applied accurately, they slip by unnoticed. The poem presents itself in grammatical units - phrases and sentences that communicate its content - and readers know exactly how to interpret the sentences because punctuation helps to make sense of them. If grammar and punctuation are mismanaged, inadequate or absent, the poem is a jumble of words. The challenge becomes to read the words in a way that makes some sort of sense, rather than marvel at the content.

If you have any doubts about grammar and punctuation, you can easily find information on them. There are websites with plenty of guidance, and there's a range of books on the subject. My own preference is to choose a book intended for children, quick to read and with simply expressed facts.

If your understanding of these mechanics of writing is comprehensive, please still take a moment to read through this list of the Big Three grammar sins.

1 Sentences lacking a main verb and its subject leave the reader dangling. Consider the following:

Sitting beneath a tree looking at the stars.

I sit beneath a tree looking at the stars.

The first sentence is incomplete, and doesn't tell the reader who is sitting there. A verb used in its present participle form with the *-ing* ending signals to the reader that there is more to come. When nothing comes, the sentence necessarily disappoints. The second sentence corrects the problem, giving a subject *I* and the main verb form *sit*.

2 When the *-ing* ending is needed, the use of the wrong verb form is equally unpleasant. *I am stood* and *she was sat* don't work in speech and sound even worse in a poem. *I am standing* and *she was sitting* are required.

3 A change of tense within a poem glares, unless there is a distinct reason for it, such as a passage in flashback and then a return to the present.

Having advised a study of grammar, I must contradict myself to mention that poetry is something of a special case. While it is important to know and understand the rules, you can occasionally produce a stunning effect by flouting them deliberately. As long as your meaning is clear and communicates itself to the reader, eccentricities of grammar may well be acceptable, even though errors are not.

Eccentricities for their own sake are an affectation. Where they work to enrich your poem, they can be enchanting. An unusual feature of style can heighten the reader's reaction.

There is one convention of grammar which may prove particularly helpful. Where a story or article breaks into a new paragraph, a poem opens a new stanza.

This is a useful point to remember when you are writing free verse. Using a set form means that you have a pattern of line and stanza breaks. It can be difficult to tell where the new stanza begins when you do not have the framework of a set form. By pinpointing the shift that would indicate a new paragraph in prose, you are going to make sense of the breaks.

Capital letters in prose occur only after a full stop or at the beginning of a proper noun. In poetry you can use a capital letter at the start of each line if you wish, regardless of the punctuation at the end of the previous line; but this is an option, not a rule, and is going out of fashion.

You will note that free verse more frequently follows the convention of prose. Your instinct will tell you whether capitals or small letters are better in the case of each individual poem.

e.e. cummings carried this option to the extreme by rejecting capital letters altogether. Neither the poetry nor the poet's status suffered, but any poet who does the same thing today might be seen as simply copying another writer's style.

Poetry allows you one form of punctuation that is unavailable in prose - the line break. In the distant past, poetry was end-stopped, punctuated at the end of every line. Writers soon tired of such a restrictive rule, and so it is totally acceptable for a line or even a stanza to end with no punctuation, but run directly on into the next line, forming an enjambment.

The tiny pause this creates, a mere suspension of breath when the poem is spoken or the fraction of a second when the eye moves to read the next line, places a very slight emphasis on the final word of the line, enabling it to be subtly highlighted.

On a very few occasions, a total absence of punctuation works. This may be useful when you wish to convey a sense of continuation, but should be seen as a rare exception rather than a generally helpful device.

EXERCISES

11 Turn on the TV or radio and write down the first phrase you hear. Use it as the trigger for a flow writing exercise, or directly to inspire a poem.

12 Put the kettle on to boil. Ask yourself what could happen to change your life in the couple of minutes it takes. It could be a telephone call, a heart attack, the arrival of a momentous letter ... Now write a detailed, specific account of everything you had to do to boil the water, and an equally detailed narrative of the life-changing moment. Draft an interleaved poem, with alternate stanzas from the first account and the second. You might left justify one set of stanzas and indent the other. This gives you the bare bones of the poem. Tinker with it, playing with the idea to produce something arresting and fascinating. Be 'green' by using the boiling water to make a nice cup of tea. When you repeat the exercise, change the task and the *what if?* list.

13 Make a list of ten clichéd similes, such as *as clean as a new pin*. Now find an original comparison to replace the clichéd one in each. Try converting the similes into metaphors.

14 Create a rainbow poem. Pick a theme, then write a short stanza on it for each colour, moving through the list from red to violet. Your theme could be something like shades of love, Christmas, memories - anything. You could take the direct approach, *Red is the colour of ...* or be more indirect, eg. *His anger smouldered a scarlet glow*.

15 Write an acrostic, where the first letter of each line of your poem spells out a 'message' when read from top to bottom. The message should be relevant to the content of the poem. Use free verse or rhyme, and if you wish start a new stanza for each new word in the message.

CHAPTER FOUR

THE POEM'S MUSIC - RHYME

For some writers, this is an essential part of the craft. For others it is anathema. The good news is that nowadays rhymers and non-rhymers are equally welcome in the world of poetry. Indeed, it is not necessary to place yourself in either of these opposing camps. It's better to decide for each poem whether it would be more effective with rhyme or in free verse. Best of all is to let the poem decide for itself.

Full rhyme involves identically pronounced stressed final vowel sounds. Although the sounds are identical, remember that spellings do not have to be the same. Full rhymes appear in *go* and *so*, but also in *hoe* and *although*, despite the fact that there is a different spelling to produce the vowel sound.

In full rhyme, anything that occurs after the final stressed vowel should also sound identical. This could be a single sound, made up of one or more letters, as in *Bid* and *lid*, or *delights* and *incites*. *Main*, *sustain* and *entertain* are full rhymes, even though there is a different number of syllables in each word, because the final stressed syllable is the one that counts.

Sometimes a whole extra unstressed syllable - or more - is present after the last stressed syllable. *Finger* and *linger* sound the same, as do *rejection* and *infection*, and *robbery* and *snobbery*. These are classed as feminine rhymes.

On the surface, the use of full rhyme appears to be the easiest device to alert readers to the fact that they are looking at a poem rather than a piece of prose. Its use is not as easy as it might seem, and fraught with traps for the unwary. Here are the five major rhyme crimes - to be avoided at all costs.

1 Producing rhyme-led material. In this, the sense or logic of the text is suspended so that the writer can make sure the words sound the same. For example, a poet might say:

> *The moon was shining high and bright,*
> *And all the stars were out that night.*
> *A nightingale began to sing......*

and from the example of the pattern set, the reader anticipates a rhyme.

> *Sweet notes to warm the dark in Spring*

or

> *His music made the woodland ring*

might be revoltingly twee, but at least they make some kind of sense. If the writer sacrificed logic for sound, we could end up with:

> *There were no bees about to sting*

or even

> *My favourite vase resembles Ming.*

These might sound like extreme examples, but still worse has been written - and the perpetrators have attempted to get it published.

2 Inversions. This is where the normal syntax of the poem has been wrenched and the word order changed to place a rhyming word at the end of a line. Examples are:

> *I searched the meadow, looked around*
> *Until a butterfly I found....*

where normal syntax would dictate the placing of the object after the subject and its associated verb, ie. *Until I found a butterfly*, and:

45

> *And while we talked and hatched our cunning plan*
> *There came into the waiting room a man....*

which should read *A man came into the waiting room.*

3   Dismal rhymes.   These are the unimaginative, predictable rhymes that have become clichés because they fit together so naturally.   It may be logical to say:

> *On Christmas Eve the girls and boys*
> *Are dreaming of their favourite toys*

and even to add:

> *With which to make a lot of noise.*

This is a case of taking the easy way out.   Search for the unexpected, and you will have created a much more memorable poem.

4   Overuse of a rhymed sound.   Each rhyme you use within a poem stands not just with the words that create the chiming sound, but beside your next example of rhyme.   Consider the effect of using full rhyme in a poem written in a number of stanzas, each of which is intended to have its own rhyming sound:

> *We all went for a picnic*
> *Upon a summer day.*
> *A swarm of wasps flew down on us*
> *And scared us all away.*

The next stanza might read:

> *We left behind the sandwiches,*
> *The biscuits, jam and cream,*
> *And ran as fast as we could go*
> *And jumped into the stream.*

The poem would be heavier and clumsier if you resorted to the same *-ay* rhyme sound you'd already used:

> *We left behind the sandwiches,*
> *The biscuits on the tray,*
> *And ran into the farmer's field*
> *And jumped into the hay.*

When you are using strict, traditional patterns of rhyme, it's also worth remembering that a word in the body of the text which chimes with the end sound is to be avoided, no matter how well it fits artistically. (The exception is, of course, when mid-line rhyming is part of the poem's regular pattern). An example of over-heavy repetition would be:

We went away with a picnic tray
Upon a summer day.

5 Breaking the pattern. When you have set a pattern for full rhyme, make sure that you use it harmoniously throughout your poem. If you start with rhyming couplets, where two consecutive lines of a poem rhyme together, you set up an expectation in the reader's mind, so that the reader anticipates the same form throughout. If you suddenly change the pattern after a dozen lines, and have alternate instead of consecutive lines rhyming, the reader feels cheated. There are a very few occasions when a break in the pattern is an integral part of the poem's structure. For example, you may be writing a poem about a carefully controlled, balanced individual, and you may be using strict rhyme and metre to reinforce your subject matter. If the character runs amok in the fourth stanza, kicks over the traces and becomes totally wild, haphazard use of metre and abandoning the rhyme could fit rather well.

Historically, poetry could be distinguished from prose by its placing of fully rhymed words at the end of lines, which were usually metrical, (as described in the next chapter), and in its earliest examples, end-stopped, with punctuation closing the line. Today poets may soften their use of full rhyme by placing it more subtly. Instead of using the end of the line, rhymes may be placed at identical or different positions within two lines. A word at the end of one line may have an internal rhyme in the same line or in another. This seems to conflict with the advice given at the end of point 4 above. In fact, it's all to do with pattern. A single example of a rhyming technique within a poem looks like a mistake. Use it repeatedly as part of the rhyme's dynamic, and it works. Let your ear and your instinct decide which is which.

The fact that full rhyme is still used gives a pleasantly harmonious air to the writing, but avoids the over emphasis on rhyming sounds that resound at the end of the lines. The same softening effect is produced by the use of enjambment, where no written punctuation appears at the line end, and the sense continues into the next line.

SET FORM RHYMING

If you are following one of the traditional forms of poetry, a few of which are described in chapter six, there will be a preordained pattern of rhyme to stick to if you want to take advantage of the dynamics of your chosen form.

Before you begin to word-in your poem, make sure that there are enough rhyming options which are compatible with your intended area of subject matter to accommodate all the rhymes you are going to need. In a terza rima, for example, you need three words that rhyme together for each sound you use. *Sea*, *tree* and *be* all rhyme together. So do *egg*, *beg* and *leg*. It is obvious that one of these sets of options would be far more difficult to place - and make sense of - in a poem than the other.

Be more vigilant the more rhyming sounds you need. Try to write a chant royal, say, and you will have to find eighteen words that rhyme together and around which you can weave a convincing poem.

Never try to place *orange*, *film* or *pint* in positions where they require a rhyme. And if you do manage to find a rhyme for any of them, award yourself a cream cake.

There are a couple of little tricks to help with rhyming. The first sounds incredibly obvious, but it's surprising how many poets won't compromise. It merely consists of changing the word for which you are struggling to find a rhyme. If the word is *chew*, for example, you might be able to change it to *eat*, *chomp* or *swallow* and find the perfect rhyme. The second is a bit more devious. It's just this. If you decide that you simply must have a particular word and the only way you can possibly rhyme it is to select a B-grade choice, a word that's almost perfect but not quite, then try to manage the lines so that the weaker word appears first. Obviously this doesn't give carte blanche to use outrageous syntax; but sometimes you can keep the integrity of the sentence structuring and meaning ... and it sounds as if the second (stronger) choice is the word you had to use to fit in. Neither of these tricks works every time, but when they do they provide a good solution.

Check out your options by using a rhyming dictionary. This is not a device for the cheat, nor does it sap your creativity and prompt you to write rhyme-led material. Rather, it is an aid to make the work of sound analysis easier. By using a rhyming dictionary you are not cheating any more than if you use a ruler to draw a straight line.

SLANT RHYME

Full rhyme chimes easily on the ear, but it is not the only way to introduce a rhyming effect into your poetry. Slant rhyme, with all its subtle variations, insinuates itself gently and resonantly. Slant rhyme depends on similarity of sounds rather than identical patterns.

The rules governing slant rhyme are few. Any similarities which can be drawn set up the effect - but because they are not obvious, it is necessary to reinforce their message by frequent use.

Slant rhyming words may be placed at the traditional end point of the line, or at any other position. Their cumulative effect is pleasing, and their use is a way to avoid any accusation that your free verse poem is no different from prose that's been chopped up and set on separate lines. (That has to be one of the most aggravating comments made to a poet, but undiscerning readers continue to make it).

The great advantage of using slant rhyme is that there are so many more words available from which you can choose. For example, take the word *larch*. Full rhymes give you few options. You could include:

arch parch march starch

Now look at the slant rhymes you could adopt:

lurch lunch latch lard lark archer marched starches shard clutch flesh lush plush staunch catch torch alarm moustache ... etc. etc.

Instinct and a sensitivity to hearing similarity of sound are the best qualifications you can have to use this style of rhyming. For interest, types of slant rhyme have been categorised:

- Assonance. This is where the same stressed vowel sound appears between different consonant sounds, eg. *crowd* rhyming with *down* or *about*.

- Alliteration. Words in close proximity begin with the same consonant sound, eg. *liquid lunch*. A tiny warning about alliteration is to try not to over-use it. A few examples here and there add to the sound effect of the poem. Too many turn it into a tonguetwister.

- Consonance. Here the consonant sound following a stressed vowel matches, eg. *thing* rhyming with *song* or *rang*.

- Full consonance. The consonant sounds on either side of a stressed vowel are the same, eg. *bat* rhyming with *but* or *boat*.

- Unaccented rhyme. Unstressed syllables at the end of words match, although the previous stressed syllable may be entirely different, eg. *butter* rhyming with *hammer* or *singer*.

- Crossed syllable rhyme. A stressed syllable in one word creates full rhyme with a differently positioned stressed syllable in another word, eg. *reflect* rhyming with *direction* or *sectional*.
- Eye rhyme. The words look as though they will sound identical, but their pronunciation is different, eg. *plough* rhyming with *cough* or *though*.
- Half rhyme. There is full rhyme in the stressed syllables of the words, but following unstressed syllables are different, eg. *haughty* rhyming with *fortieth* or *portliness*.
- Synthetic rhyme. This is where pronunciation or natural stress has to be wrenched in order to produce the appearance of full rhyme, eg. *harebell* rhyming with *expel* or *foretell*.

Just to add a hint of confusion, not all books agree on the terminology, and different patterns of slant rhyme appear under different names. The important point to remember is that similarity of sound creates the poetry effect in free verse.

A free verse poem suffused with examples of slant rhyme, not just at line ends but all through the text, has a powerfully poetic sound. The use of just a few slant rhymes within a fully-rhymed poem enhances its poetic quality.

EXERCISES

16 Write a poem about yourself from the viewpoint of an animal ... maybe a pampered pet, or a spider you have just evicted from the bath. Let its voice and personality speak out. When you return to this exercise, try it again in the voice of your car, a piece of jewellery, a cup.

17 Take a poem you wrote some time ago. Look at every word in it, asking yourself if you can find a more appropriate alternative to communicate your message more efficiently. Then check whether you could change it to enrich the poem, either with slant rhyme or with more onomatopoeic vocabulary.

18 Find a short poem (about 16 lines) written by another poet. Read it aloud several times. Start with a 'straight' reading, then read it more quickly and more slowly. Say it in a range of dialects. Exaggerate the use of onomatopoeia. All this may seem to have no practical application, but it helps you appreciate the poem more fully and demonstrates the way different readings change the dynamics of a poem. It also helps you to comprehend how other readers will interpret your poem. It's a good idea to wait until you're on your own to do this. Otherwise you'll be teased mercilessly or bundled into a straitjacket.

19 Devise a scurrilous verse about someone you dislike either personally or by repute. It's cathartic.

20 Write a holiday-based poem in any style you wish. It may be a travelogue of exotic places, a detailed look at some famous landmark, a moan about a place you didn't want to go to - (if you've no inspiration for that one, talk to a teenager) - a witty verse monologue listing all the disasters encountered.

CHAPTER FIVE

THE POEM'S MUSIC - RHYTHM

Rhythm surrounds every part of our lives. Before we are born we are comforted by the regular throb of our mother's heartbeat, and as babies we are reassured by being rocked back and forth. There is rhythm in the pulsing of blood around the body, the changing motions of the earth producing day and night cycles, and the passage of the seasons. There is rhythm in the regularity of the tide, the waxing and waning of the moon, in the wave patterns through which light and sound travel.

It's not surprising that poetry, which is close to the roots of existence, should be full of rhythm, the flow of stressed and unstressed syllables through language.

Perhaps more than rhyme, rhythm makes poetry memorable for its speaker and holds the attention of the listener, which were vital considerations in the days of the oral tradition. But as well as being useful as a means of prompting memory and gripping an audience, a pleasing rhythm quite simply makes words more attractive to listen to.

Think about it from the angle of a toddler. Small children learn to apply the skills of language through rhythm. As soon as youngsters can pronounce recognisable words and phrases, they start to learn nursery rhymes, many of which are accompanied by regular movements, such as *Pat-a-cake baker's man, See-saw Margery Daw*. The strong rhythms instil an element of fun. And while the children play, they are practising memory techniques, handling vocabulary, absorbing cadences of their language with its stressed and unstressed syllables, and discovering grammatical constructions.

Apart from the fun bit, there is also an innate power in rhythm, which throbs in our mind and reverberates through our imagination. Traditionally, chants and incantations have been used to invoke magical or supernatural responses. A strongly rhythmical piece, however short, puts its message across. Countless consumer products are advertised with rhythmic slogans.

Rhythm maintains the intensity of a poem, carrying it from writer to reader. The writer's intentions are less likely to be misunderstood if appropriate rhythms flow through the poem. Rhythm also reinforces the subject matter and applies a specific tone to the piece. It is part of the music of poetry, and has the power to move and excite as well as narrate a story or create an atmosphere.

As well as contributing to its music, rhythm is part of the completeness of the poem. Its insistence tells you that there is more to come, and its ultimate and satisfying conclusion rounds the poem strongly and beautifully.

METRE

A strict measurement of the flow of poetry is the pattern of its beats or metre. The art of applying metre to a poem is a bit like the art of training a dog. When you first meet each other, you may both be wary and anxious. The dog leaps about all over the place, and the idea of keeping it under control is reminiscent of King Canute and the unpleasantness with the tide. But of course, eventually you get used to each other, you assume command, and the apparently untamable animal trots happily by your side, and quickly becomes your best friend.

Here's the good news. While metre does have its complications, you can jog along quite satisfactorily with only one aspect of it in your control. If you can count to five and understand the dynamics of an iamb, a.k.a. iambus, you have the wherewithal to write a huge range of set forms of poetry. Adding a little at a time, you can extend your range of knowledge and be able to work out the metre of all the other forms.

One iamb consists of two syllables, the first being unstressed and the second stressed. This *ti-tum* is the rhythm of the heartbeat, which may explain why a line of iambs has such a pleasing, almost comforting effect. An iamb may consist of two words or a single word of two syllables, eg:

a car

before

In a line of poetry, iambs can be shared by different words throughout the line, eg:

The quality of mercy is not strained

so the first syllable of *quality* completes the first iambic foot, and the first syllable of *mercy* the third.

This line from *The Merchant of Venice* is an example of iambic pentameter, or five iambic feet. (That's why you have to be able to count up to five). It appears throughout Shakespeare's plays, in Milton's Paradise Lost and in Wordsworth's The Prelude. It's the metrical form of the sonnet, and a comfortable, easy metre to use. Unrhymed iambic pentameter is, in fact, one of the set forms of poetry, blank verse - not to be confused with free verse, which has no set metre.

If there are just four iambic feet in the line, the metrical pattern is referred to as iambic tetrameter, and that's another popular metre. Iambic hexameter, also referred to as an alexandrine, takes six iambs to the line.

There's one point to remember whenever you are writing in iambs. Every line should begin with an unstressed syllable. If you make sure you start with this, and continue the alternating stress pattern throughout the line, you can't go wrong. There's just one exception mentioned below.

Here's a mini-exercise to try your hand with iambic feet.

1 Which of these words is an iambic foot?

anxious   *ready*   *evolve*

2 Why are the other two not?

3 Divide this line of iambic pentameter into separate feet. Mark *x* above an unstressed syllable, / above a stressed one:

A steady mind controls a steady hand.

4 What is the metre of this line?

Explain yourself, you wicked boy!

Check your answers at the end of this chapter, just before the five exercises.

If you enjoy working with metre, here's a table giving the names of the most common metrical feet with an explanation and example, and another listing the terms for line length in feet.

FOOT NAME	EXPLANATION	EXAMPLE
iamb/iambus	unstressed followed by stressed syllable	*again*
trochee	stressed followed by unstressed syllable	*darling*
pyrrhic	two unstressed syllables	*in a*
spondee	two stressed syllables	*cart horse*
dactyl	one stressed, two unstressed	*octopus*
anapaest	two unstressed, one stressed	*on a bus*
bacchic	one unstressed, two stressed	*in green fields*
anti-bacchic	two stressed, one unstressed	*strange meeting*
amphimacer	one stressed, one unstressed, one stressed	*go to sleep*
amphibrach	one unstressed, one stressed, one unstressed	*deportment*

| molossus | three stressed | *cold dark night* |
| tribrach | three unstressed | *if it is* |

NAME OF LINE LENGTH	NUMBER OF FEET
monometer	one foot to the line
dimeter	two feet
trimeter	three feet
tetrameter	four feet
pentameter	five feet
hexameter	six feet
heptameter	seven feet
octameter	eight feet

On the other hand, if all this seems deadly dull and boring, don't panic. Recognition of the terms in which metre is described is useful. An understanding of the composition of feet may help you to write poetry. But there is a far more important factor than the mathematical ability to follow all this. That is the poet's ear.

Much that is connected with writing poetry is instinctive. Choice and treatment of subjects, word selection and comprehension of slant rhyme are all achieved by the ear and the heart rather than the head. The same is true of metre. If you have any sense of the musicality of poetry, you will know automatically if you have used the wrong foot, or created the wrong number of feet in a line. It will glare at you, demanding that you put it right.

When you feel absolutely confident about your ease in handling metre, remember that you can bring neat counterpoint into your writing by making occasional use of variations within it.

A line of iambic pentameter, for example, can be enhanced by the substitution of a trochee for an iambus as the first foot, (initial trochaic substitution - and this is the exception mentioned earlier). To stay with Shakespeare, an example of this occurs in *A Midsummer Night's Dream*, where Titania advises Bottom:

Out of this wood do not desire to go:

The first foot is the iamb's mirror image, with a stressed syllable followed by an unstressed, and then the other four feet of the line revert to the usual iambs.

The other frequently used variant is the feminine ending, which brings an additional, unstressed syllable to the end of a line, creating an attractive effect. The eponymous hero of *Hamlet* has one at the start of his great soliloquy:

To be, or not to be: that is the question:

When you are adding variety to your work in this way, always be sure that you are making an artistically motivated decision to do so. Don't ever change the expected metrical pattern because your own ineptitude prevents you from producing a fully metrical line. Again, trust your instinct.

You may be thinking that instinct has to be born in you, and cannot be achieved. I honestly believe that the poet's instinct is inherent in each of us - but that we need to work on it and hone it until it is functioning to optimum capacity.

The best way to nurture instinct in writing poetry is to read it. Successful poets are likely to spend more time reading the poetry of others than writing their own.

MINI EXERCISE ANSWERS

1 *Evolve.*
2 *Anxious* and *ready* are both composed of a stressed syllable followed by an unstressed, so they are trochees rather than iambs.
3 x / x /   x / x / x /
   A steady mind controls a steady hand.
4 Iambic tetrameter.

EXERCISES

21 Starting with the phrase *I remember*, write a list poem about your teenage years. You could focus on interests, favourite foods, shopping, following a sport - or create a collage of memories spanning different themes.

22 Think of a regular metrical tune with a strong beat. (A hymn tune is ideal). Now create your own words to the pattern of the tune, with exactly the right number of syllables and the identical pattern of stressed and unstressed sounds in each line. If appropriate, you can replicate rhyme placings too.

23 Recalling the phrase *Be careful what you wish for*, imagine that your dearest dream came true. Would it change your life? If so, how? What would it really be like to have achieved your dream? Is there a downside? Craft a free verse poem from a reality check on the situation.

24 Treat yourself to a collection of contemporary poetry for children. A librarian or the head of young readers' section in a bookshop will give you guidance if this is unfamiliar territory. Read and relish the contents, making mental comparisons between today's poetry and the work you read as a child in primary school. Is the poetry better or less inspiring than the poems you knew in childhood? What problems face today's writer for children? Could you write poetry like the work in the collection?

25 Write a poem in any form based on an irrational fear. Leave the end open to hint at some unnamed menace.

CHAPTER SIX

TAKING SHAPE

As soon as you start writing words onto paper, a shape begins to emerge, even if it is only the pattern of notes spread across the page. It is important to be sensitive to this shape. Your initial response may be dictated by instinct, and already anticipating a suitable layout for the poem.

So at this early stage, the eventual length of the poem and form it will take are beginning to appear. Remember, though, that there is still a long way to go. If you strive to treat the emerging shape as if it is set in stone, you may find that your writing becomes stilted and restricted. Keep your mind open to the range of possibilities you will encounter. It could be that the initial structure needs to be re-thought as you accumulate additional material.

You may complete a first draft of the poem and then realise that your pattern is not right. Be prepared to go back to the drawing board and start again. This is not as daunting a task as it may sound. After all, you now have words on paper. There's a saying - *first get it written, then get it right*. You can play with the words you've set down, changing their patterns at will, until you find the structure which is most appropriate for that particular poem.

Over hundreds of years, patterns of poetry have emerged which have proved to be good strong vehicles for delivering the poem's message. These originated all over the world, and have been adapted for use in a range of languages. They continue to evolve, as today's writers modify the forms to suit their own voice, or devise new ones to suit a specific idea.

A poem which presents itself in one of these forms is easier to mould than one that does not come in such a pattern. A set form provides the external framework onto which the body of the poem may be fitted. A free verse poem, on the other hand, has a skeleton of empty space, and the poem's flesh develops out of and around it.

Within any set form, the dynamics of that form dictate the finished shape. If your material is leading you into writing a sonnet, for example, you know from the outset that it will have fourteen lines of ten syllables each in iambic pentameter, and a set pattern of rhymes. Although it is wise to keep in the back of your mind the possibility that there may be a better vehicle for the idea, the task of structuring the poem has been simplified.

If no set form presents itself alongside the idea, you will need to think carefully about the pattern that will be best for it. Look again - and this time more carefully - at your notes. Do they divide themselves naturally into sections? These could be stanza divisions. Is there any discernible pattern in their positioning on the paper? Indentations - lines offset from the left margin - might be indicated. Does the material stand as a solid block? It could be that the poem needs a similarly solid structure.

The more you build on your writing, the more you need to be aware of the developing shape, until you find you are moulding form even as you are selecting the words and images to convey your message.

SOME POPULAR FORMS

Each form is accompanied by a note of its metrical requirement and rhyme pattern. For the latter, this notation is used:

First sound to appear that will rhyme	a
Second sound to appear that will rhyme	b
Third sound to appear that will rhyme	c
A word or whole line that is repeated uses upper case:	
Repeated word/line rhyming with first sound	A
If more than one word/line is repeated rhyming with first sound	A1, A2, A3
Repeated word/line rhyming with second sound	B
If more than one word/line is repeated	B1, B2, B3
Refrain	R
Line that has no rhyme	x

Confused? You will be. But it's easier to follow this pattern when you see it with examples. If you're still confused by the end, try a couple of glasses of wine and read it again. It may not make any more sense, but you'll feel better.

QUATRAIN FORMS

A four line poem, or a four line stanza within a longer poem, is referred to as a quatrain. This is a convenient and simple form to use, and a vehicle that can be adapted to suit a range of ideas.

You can produce quatrains in any line length and metre you wish, and they provide fertile ground for experimentation to explore the effectiveness of your idea. Remember that a regular line length or pattern of line lengths should be sustained throughout once it has been set at the beginning of the poem. If you want to use irregular line lengths, make sure you do this from the outset, rather than raising the reader's expectations falsely.

A quatrain can consist of two rhyming couplets, using a rhyme pattern of:

a a b b

Around the garden, through the bower	a
A ghost walked at the midnight hour.	a
He wailed a tragic cry to me -	b
'Come, say a prayer and set me free.'	b

Couplets look simple, but are actually quite a difficult style of rhyme to work with. You have very little room to manoeuvre between the two rhyming sounds, while ensuring that you are making sense and that your chosen line length and metre are observed.

Couplets are useful, however, in comic poetry, and a large number of couplets strung together can make a lighthearted verse monologue. Regularity and accuracy of rhyme and metre are essential if a humorous verse is to work - humour is less forgiving than other themes.

Alternating the rhymes gives you that little bit more leeway to put your message across. You can have just the second and fourth lines rhyming:

x a x a

or you can rhyme first and third lines as well as second and fourth:

a b a b

Leaf filtered sunlight dappled on the path,	x
Turned day to twilight deep inside the wood.	a
My heart was beating fast with fear, I rushed	x
Back to the normal world I understood.	a

or

Leaf filtered sunlight fell; the way was hushed;	a
Day turned to twilight deep inside the wood.	b

My heart was beating fast with fear, I rushed   a
Back to the normal world I understood.   b

One pleasing set form of quatrains with alternate rhymes is the ballad stanza. As its name suggests, this is a good pattern for conveying a narrative. The story flows along with ease. The rhyme pattern for this stanza is:

    x a x a

The unrhymed first and third lines of the stanza are written in iambic tetrameter. The rhymed second and fourth lines are in iambic trimeter.

Most precious sight to every salt   x
  Who sailed the Spanish Main   a
Was Blackrock Island's lighthouse beam   x
  That lit him home again;   a

Until one night a pirate ship   x
  Fetched up in Lighthouse Cove,   b
Whose vicious crew were seeking sites   x
  To bury treasure trove.   b

These pirate curs, with cruel intent,   x
  Were watching from the deck,   c
And knew the rocky ocean floor   x
  Could cause a ship to wreck.   c

A sometimes neglected quatrain is the Italian envelope stanza. This is written in iambic pentameter. One pair of rhyming lines is wrapped around a rhyming couplet:

    a b b a

His face was set. He wore an evil leer.   a
His victim stood before him, brave and calm,   b
Not knowing why the other wished him harm,   b
And hiding any trace of doubt or fear.   a

In the rubai, (plural rubais or rubayat), the effect is produced by rhyming the first, second and fourth lines of the quatrain, while the third is unrhymed:

a a x a

This is an Arabic form, which uses iambic pentameter or iambic tetrameter.

His voice soared through the stifling heat of day.	a
We could not see the singer, for he lay	a
Spreadeagled on the salted, net-strewn board.	x
His boat bobbed on the waves across the bay.	a

A variant of this form is the linking version known as interlocking rubayat. Here, the sound at the end of the third line becomes the main rhyme for the next stanza:

a a b a   b b c b   c c d c   d d e d   etc.

His voice soared through the stifling heat of day.	a
We could not see the singer, for he lay	a
Spreadeagled on the salted, net-strewn board.	b
His boat bobbed on the waves across the bay.	a
And as we watched he sat upright, explored	b
The wide horizon, threw a length of cord	b
With floats to mark positions on the sea.	c
We left the beach and walked away, restored	b
By witnessing this idyll, and the free	c
..........etc.	

After any number of quatrains, the final stanza in interlocking rubayat picks up the rhyme of the first line in the poem, creating a pattern of   z z a z   (z representing the final rhyme sound selected, not that you have to have 26 stanzas)!

THE SONNET

This is by no means the easiest form - in fact, it's one of the most difficult to write well - but it is particularly attractive and repays the effort expended to produce it.

It started in Italy as a *sonetto*, a little song, during the thirteenth century. The form has fourteen lines of iambic pentameter. Originally it was divided into eight lines (an octave) and six (a sestet) with a distinct shift of emphasis - the turn - between these line groups. The octave suggests an idea and the sestet offers a new slant on it or some different impulse of thought. A line may be left between the two sections, or the sonnet may read as a single block of text.

The octave creates an envelope effect in its rhyme scheme:

a b b a a b b a

Because the two 'envelopes' use the same vowel sounds, there is a particular unity to the lines.

The sestet takes different patterns. In its basic form, an Italian (also known as Petrarchan) sonnet concludes:

c d c d c d   or   c d e c d e

CAVE OF THE SYBIL, NAPLES

Walk quietly here, for here the Sybil walked	a
in passages where Cumans dared not go.	b
Her whispered words of prophecy would flow	b
through pentagons of light where tunnels forked.	a
Her truth was never doubted; when she talked	a
a nation stopped to listen, had to know	b
each utterance. They begged her to bestow	b
good fortune where the gravest portents stalked.	a
Walk quietly here, for here the tourists tread	c
their sacrilege within a sacred place	d
which Virgil honoured, modern man defiles.	e

No one can know for sure the ghosts have fled,   c
the mysteries dissolved: and in this space,   d
the Sybil's whisper haunts us still, beguiles.   e

The sonnet was introduced to England in the sixteenth century, and a succession of poets adapted the form, most notably by altering the pattern of the sestet. Wordsworth had a whale of a time with it, eg:

c d e d c e
c d d c d c
c d c d e e
c d d e c e

Milton dispensed with the formality of the break in mood at the end of the octave, and placed this pivotal point within or at the end of a line somewhere around the eighth or ninth.

A more radical change, though, was brought about by a number of sixteenth century writers. It bears William Shakespeare's name, not because he was the first poet to use it, but arguably the best.

The English, Elizabethan or Shakespearean sonnet has a much longer opening phase. Twelve lines deliver the meat of the poem, and then a rhyming couplet rounds and seals it. The fourteen line iambic pentameter pattern remains intact, but the new rhyme scheme is:

a b a b c d c d e f e f g g

MONA LISA

All visitors to Paris ought to see   a
the treasures of the Louvre. We stood in lines,   b
slow shifting for a glimpse, to say that we   a
could not be branded hopeless Philistines.   b
The soft-shoe-shuffle edged us, ten-deep, past   c
La Giaconda, while a bored guard yelled   d
Non, pas de flash! as shutters clicked, and burst   /c
of light attacked the patina. Propelled   d

by sweating crowds, we *ooh'd* and *aah'd* to note	e
the picture's age, small size, its tiny frame	f
encompassing the famous smile, remote	e
but redolent with latent passion's flame.	f
And, strangely, here on Paris streets we know	g
that face will watch us everywhere we go.	g

In a game of Spot the Deliberate Mistake, you will have noticed that the seventh line uses a slant rhyme for variety. This is a perfectly acceptable practice, as long as there is enough similarity in its sounds for the poem not to lose ground in the rhyming stakes.

So how much is enough? Unfortunately, there's no sensible answer to this one. You have to trust your instinct, your eye and your ear. If you are in doubt about the effectiveness of any variant, or if you know that it's there only because you couldn't think of a word to fit exactly - cut it out and start again. If you can say, hand on heart, that it was added for its pleasing sound, keep it in.

The breakthrough of this new form of sonnet brought an important advantage with it. Because of differences between the Italian and the English language, Italian offers a lot more options for rhyming words than English does. The Petrarchan sonnet needs four rhymes that will fit the poem - and make sense - for each of the two rhyming sounds that are used in the octave. The Shakespearean sonnet never has more than two words rhyming together.

It is interesting to note that a variation on the latter devised by Spenser has not caught on - probably because he returned to a repeated pattern of rhymes that demands as many lines rhyming with the same sounds as the Petrarchan form. His rhyme scheme is:

a b a b b c b c c d c d e e

AMERICAN SONNET PATTERNS

In recent times, American writers have made some exciting explorations of the sonnet form. The Visser sonnet follows the form of the Italian sonnet, but instead of placing all the rhyming words at the line ends, many are scattered internally, within the lines.

A Foster sonnet makes more use of the rhyming couplet idea, and takes this pattern:

a b c c a a b b d d e e f f

The Mason sonnet makes even more use of the same rhyme sounds than the Italian, with the scheme:

a b c a b c c b d b a d d a

The Beymorlin sonnet is the most fiendish I have ever come across. Not only does it bear any traditional set of sonnet rhymes at the end of the lines: it has an extra set of rhymes at the beginning, which may or may not follow the same scheme as the line-end rhymes. Rhyme may occur within the first two syllables of the line.

To aid the annotation, I have named the initial rhymes a, b, c etc. and the line-end rhymes m, n, o.

SEEING DAVID HOCKNEY'S: 'A BIGGER SPLASH'

a	Blue water glimmers, mirrored in blue sky	m
b	Where sun, unseen, sends brilliant glow of heat.	n
a	Two palms, unbending, fan green fronds on high.	m
b	Air sweats with August where bright colours meet.	n
c	Reflected shapes make window-image show	o
d	To prove that there is life beyond the frame,	p
c	Expected guests and furnished overflow,	o
d	A moving pattern fixed to forge the game.	p
e	Real motion is the aftermath of plunge.	q
f	A swimmer scythes pool surface. Shooting spray	r
e	Steals rainbows for each crystal. Fountains lunge	q

f	And glimmer, glisten, prismed as they play.	r
g	Brash-coloured, angular, bold-stroked and free,	s
g	'Splash' reaches from the canvas; drenches me.	s

THE VILLANELLE

This form originated in France, beginning life as a song with refrains but without a fixed pattern. It may have been used as a dance or work chant, often with a rustic theme, and the pattern we know today was fixed in the early 1600s. It's a particularly haunting form of poetry, where the first and third lines of the poem recur in an almost incantatory fashion, but are brought together for the only time at the very end of the piece.

The modern villanelle is usually written in iambic pentameter or iambic tetrameter. The poem consists of any odd number of three-line stanzas, (tercets), with five being the most popular, followed by a single quatrain. The rhyme scheme is:

A1 b A2   a b A1   a b A2   a b A1   a b A2   etc. ending a b A1 A2

BOY KING

They bound your body with exquisite care,	A1
performed the rites that fortified your end.	b
We ripped you from your tomb and laid you bare.	A2

Four perfect jars were sanctified to share	a
the burden of your viscera. To mend	b
they bound your body, with exquisite care	A1

wound bandages, anointed, offered prayer,	a
made you in death their deity and friend.	b
We ripped you from your tomb and laid you bare.	A2

We severed limbs and hacked your torso; hair,	a
nails, bones were analysed. We can't pretend.	b
They bound your body with exquisite care;	A1
we stripped your dignity, not knowing where	a
your anger would erupt, your curse descend.	b
We ripped you from your tomb and laid you bare	A2
of amulets' protection, unaware	a
your vengeance would pursue us to our end.	b
They bound your body with exquisite care.	A1
We ripped you from your tomb and laid you bare.	A2

You might have noticed that one of the 'b' lines does not bear the usual rhyme, but is a repetition of a word used previously. This is not, of course, the standard form: but in this case, the desire to parallel *your end* in the first stanza with *our end* in the last made it seem appropriate. Is that acceptable? Poetry isn't an exact science. It's up to every individual to decide.

There are occasions when it is necessary to alter the wording of the refrain lines slightly in order to make sense of the poem, but this technique should be applied sparingly. The grammar and punctuation, on the other hand, can be varied as much as you wish, adding a fresh slant to the repeated lines.

Do remember when you embark on writing a villanelle that you will have to find a lot of rhymes for each of two sounds; and that your refrain lines will have to make sense when you place them next to each other at the end of the poem. If you reach the final couplet and then discover that the two lines make a nonsense when placed consecutively, you have big problems.

In any form where repetition is used, it is pleasing if the poem can be seen to have moved on between repeats, so that the repeat has an added nuance of meaning. This presents extraordinary difficulties for our next form.

THE PANTOUM

Of Malayan origin, the pantoum was brought into Europe early in the nineteenth century, and takes the incantatory effect a stage further. It is usually written in iambic tetrameter or iambic pentameter, and consists of any number of quatrains, each line of which is repeated in its entirety. It takes the pattern:

A1 B1 A2 B2   B1 C1 B2 C2   C1 D1 C2 D2   D1 E1 D2 E2 etc.

ending with a stanza which draws in the first rhyming lines in reverse order:

Z1 A2 Z2 A1

or with a final couplet that reverses the first rhyming lines:

Y1 Z1 Y2 Z2   A2 A1

ALONE TOGETHER

No ghosts disturb the silence of this place.	A1
I gaze across the tide's relentless flow.	B1
I watch the clouds, but only see your face	A2
etched on the sky and rippling below.	B2
I gaze across the tide's relentless flow	B1
While memories like snapshots fill my head	C1
etched on the sky and rippling below.	B2
I cannot say aloud that you are dead.	C2
While memories like snapshots fill my head	C1
my arms are throbbing with the need for you.	D1
I cannot say aloud that you are dead,	C2
for everywhere your essence urges through.	D2

My arms are throbbing with the need for you.   D1
I watch the clouds, but only see your face,   A2
for everywhere your essence urges through.   D2
No ghosts disturb the silence of this place.   A1

As with the villanelle, new use of grammar and punctuation is applauded, but variations in the actual wording of the lines should be applied with caution. The most graphic description I have ever heard of the business of writing pantoums is that *it does your head in.*

THE LIMERICK

For a little light relief after some heavy forms, the limerick is fun, quick and easy to produce, and provides an excellent medium for being rude about your friends. Just five lines long, it consists of a first, second and last line that rhyme together, and a shorter third and fourth line that rhyme, in the pattern:

    a a b b a

A shrewish young lady called Kate	a
Put her Dad in a terrible bate.	a
She wouldn't get wed -	b
Said she'd rather be dead	b
Till Petruchio made her his mate.	a

You can employ as much latitude as you wish with the limerick. Its rhythm is more important than a consideration of metre, but the rhythm needs to work flawlessly if the humour is to be present.

There's a long tradition of using coarse subject matter in this form, so feel free to be as smutty as you like for adult readers.

THE TRIOLET

This is an attractive little form of just eight lines, which originated in France. The first, fourth and seventh lines are the same, and the eighth line is a repeat of the second. The usual metrical pattern is iambic trimeter, tetrameter or pentameter, but other feet may be used as long as all lines in the poem are the same length and style. The rhyme scheme is:

A B a A a b A B

POET SISTERS

My sister, writing in a time and place	A
I never can inhabit, think of me.	B
Our fates are fettered, locked in close embrace,	a
my sister. Writing in a time and place	A
my mortal span denies, you learn the space	a
I knew, explore it, soaring wild and free.	b
My sister, writing in a time and place	A
I never can inhabit, think of me.	B

This is a good vehicle for a light, cameo poem, as well as for more thought-provoking material.

THE MINUTE

The minute is a modern form devised in America, and based on the idea of a single minute in time. It consists of sixty syllables, representing the seconds. There are twelve lines, all of which are iambic, lines one, five and nine being tetrameters and the rest dimeters. The lines rhyme in couplets:

a a b b c c d d e e f f

The subject of the poem should be something that occurs in the space of one minute. Its punctuation should be that of prose, so capital letters are only used for proper nouns or to start a new sentence.

PYROMANIA

I love to watch a flame flare bright.	a
In search of light	a
I strike a match	b
and note the catch	b
of spark to paper, prompting me	c
to fan, and see	c
the flames leap higher,	d
ignite a fire	d
A minute - less - a golden tongue	e
leaps out among	e
my papers, claims	f
my room in flames.	f

One little point about this example: the 'd' rhyme sound may seem too long for the line. The *-ire* sound is, of course, a triphthong, or triple-sounding vowel. Although it is strictly classified as a single syllable, some speakers would make it sound like two. If you use one of these iffy vowels, be aware of the fact that the voice can influence your syllable count.

THE RONDEAU

The rondeau is one of a number of French forms that use few different rhyming sounds (two in this case) and also repetition to create their effect. A rondeau has fifteen lines written in three stanzas, the last line of the second and third stanzas being a refrain that picks up the first word or phrase of the poem.

Lines may be of any single length and metre (except for the shorter refrain lines), and the popular iambic tetrameter and pentameter are seen most frequently. The rhyme scheme is:

a a b b a   a a b R   a a b b a R

SIGN OF BETRAYAL

One golden rose was all you gave, a sign	a
I would ignore, but know I must define.	a
A true love's roses are forever red,	b
while yellow shows your love for me is dead,	b
where bloom and thorns are tied with silken twine.	a
An age ago you poured me honeyed wine,	a
made sweeter promises. You now consign	a
our memories to dust, offer instead	b
one golden rose.	R
I used to think our love could redesign	a
the universe; but though your words were fine,	a
betrayal lay in words that were unsaid.	b
Your gift is token that all hope is dead	b
and tells the world you are no longer mine -	a
one golden rose.	R

These are not the easiest of poems to write, but the form is attractive and pleasing.

THE RONDEL

This is a medieval French form, and although early rondels are found in English poetry, they became popular in the nineteenth century. The rondel also has just two rhyming sounds, and the first and second lines of the poem are refrains. There are fourteen lines of any single length and metre, divided into three stanzas, and they rhyme:

    A B b a   a b A B   a b b a A B   or   A B a b   b a A B
a b a b A B

14th APRIL, 1912

The people thought their rescuers would come.	A
This ship was safer than the frozen sea,	B
so passengers ignored the Captain's plea.	b
Unsinkable, this ship would not succumb.	a
Ripped open by the ice, she still had some	a
faint hope of floating. They would soon be free,	b
the people thought. The rescuers would come,	A
this ship was safer than the frozen sea.	B
Iced inrush jarred her equilibrium	a
until she foundered. Then too late to flee	b
her passengers screamed their last agony,	b
fell silent as a black flood struck them dumb.	a
The people thought their rescuers would come -	A
this ship was safer than the frozen sea.	B

There is a thirteen line version of this form, which works in the same way but repeats only one or the other of the refrain lines at the end, rather than both.

THE RHYMED SESTINA

This is one of those forms that looks as though it will be horrendous. And it is. But it's a terrific challenge, beloved of crossword fanatics and jigsaw puzzlers as well as poets. It is 39 lines long, and consists of six sestets and an envoi of three lines.

It is based on six words using two rhyming sounds, and they appear as the final words of each line of the poem in a predetermined order that creates a pattern of rhymes in alternate lines. In the envoi all six words appear, one within and one at the end of each line. The sestina may be written in any single line length and metre, and iambic pentameter is favoured by many poets. The line sequence is as follows:

Line	Repeat	Line	Repeat	
1	A	19	B	
2	B	20	E	
3	C	21	F	
4	D	22	A	
5	E	23	D	
6	F	24	C	
7	F	25	C	
8	A	26	B	
9	D	27	A	
10	C	28	F	
11	B	29	E	
12	E	30	D	
13	E	31	D	
14	F	32	C	
15	A	33	B	
16	D	34	E	
17	C	35	F	
18	B	36	A	
		37	A	D
		38	B	C
		39	E	F

LESSON

They taunted him, and mocked him for a fool;   A
he let resentment simmer, fester, grow.   B
Who would have thought his 'friends' could be so cruel?   C
And which of those tormenting youths could know   D
the scheme he nurtured; take a gun to school,   E
defeat the bullies with a single blow.   F

Each jibe held power to bruise, a body blow   F
for one who knew that he was not a fool   A
in spite of all their jeering. There was no   D
escape for him from vicious tongues and cruel   C
abuse. He knew he must ignore, or grow   B
a thicker skin to carry him through school.   E

Nobody listened. No one in the school   E
could shield him from his suffering, or blow   F
the wicked words away. He played the fool,   A
a desperate act, so everyone would know -   D
or guess - he shrugged his pain aside; a cruel   C
pretence - ignoring only made it grow.   B

The gun was in his shirt. He felt it grow   B
in his imagination till the school   E
was scarcely big enough to hold it. 'Blow   F
them all away,' he muttered, 'watch this fool   A
show how I choose to let them live, or know   D
my fear, my agony. I can be cruel   C

as any of them, wicked, vile and cruel   C
enough to threaten, watch their terror grow,   B
eliminate them. Not bad for a fool.'   A
And he became a vast colossus, blow   F
by blow annihilating half the school   E
- it seemed - as trickling blood formed rivers. 'No,   D

Oh no!' he wailed and screamed and sobbed, 'Oh no!'	D
He'd only wanted them to stop, not cruel	C
revenge. He'd thought the gun would make them grow	B
to care, respect him. Too late now. The school	E
would not recover from this savage blow.	F
He knew he'd blundered, proved himself the fool.	A

But this was real. No fooling now. And no	A	D
forgiveness, just a growing pit, a cruel	B	C
revenge. And school would deal the final blow.	E	F

Just when you thought you were on top of the form, along comes another pattern to knock you back. This is the unrhymed sestina; and its little trick is to change the order of the repeated lines. In this case, as the name suggests, there is no rhyme but just that all-important set of six line-end words. The pattern is:

Line	Repeat	Line	Repeat
1	A	19	E
2	B	20	C
3	C	21	B
4	D	22	F
5	E	23	A
6	F	24	D
7	F	25	D
8	A	26	E
9	E	27	A
10	B	28	C
11	D	29	F
12	C	30	B
13	C	31	B
14	F	32	D

15	D	33	F
16	A	34	E
17	B	35	C
18	E	36	A

37	B	E
38	D	C
39	F	A

Unrhymed sestinas are more popular than the rhymed variety; but they are just as tricky to write.

THE DIZAIN

Another form that originated in France, a dizain has ten lines of iambic tetrameter or pentameter, and has a deliciously enclosed and finished feel with its neat, mirror-imaged rhyme scheme:

a b a b b c c d c d

MERMAID

She bathes in moonlight, leans against a rock	a
and combs her golden waterfall of hair.	b
Her breasts gleam pewter, hips are sequinned shock,	a
their scaly taper ending in a flare	b
of cloven tail. Her lips entice. Beware.	b
Beware the lure of siren song she sings	c
to drag the sailors to her when sea flings	c
its wildest waves to pound upon the shore.	d
She promises enchantment; only brings	c
destruction - drowning on the ocean floor.	d

Because of its brief pattern, this form is not, perhaps, the best vehicle through which to convey weighty subject matter, but is good for delicate descriptive purposes, and can pack a punch when required.

THE TERZA RIMA

One of the neatest of set forms, this 'third rhyme' pattern originated in Italy, and consists of a number of tercets and then a final line or couplet. It is usually written in iambic pentameter. There is a chain rhyming effect, linking the stanzas together by means of the middle line of each rhyming with the first and third lines of the next. The final line or couplet rhymes with the middle line of the final tercet.

a b a   b c b   c d c   d e d   e f e ......etc. until   y z y   z
or   y z y   z z

THE DANCE REHEARSAL - Degas

Such movement and such stillness side by side   a
convey the atmosphere no photograph   b
could ever capture. Ballerinas glide,   a

reflecting angles of the spiral path   /b
ascending from the studio. Some rest   c
with careless grace downstage, and talk and laugh.   b

The choreographer exacts the best   c
performance each can give; sparing with praise,   d
he frowns, refusing to appear impressed.   c

Long windows slide the morning sun's warm rays   d
across the floor, refracting prismed light   e
through tulle and lace, kaleidoscope displays.   d

A swirl of sashes, satin shoes, silk tights   /e
completes the costume. Hair's a knotted mane   f

upon each head in elegance of height.   e

Stand at the picture; sense its size, the grain   f
of texture, shape, and weight before the call   g
to day-job duties draws you once again.   f

Then, leaving, keep a place in memory full   /g
of dancers, whose remembered image gleams   h
to lighten dismal moments with recall -   g

to live and dance again within your dreams.   h

You will note that there are some slant rhyme variations within this poem, where *path* rhymes with *photograph* and *laugh*, *tights* rhymes with *light* and *height*, and *full* rhymes with *call* and with its repeated sound in *recall*.

The decision to create these tiny slants in the rhyme pattern was made to add some variety to the material. Here again, their acceptability is recognised by instinct. I believe that these slants work - but you may have different ideas.

The terza rima is an adaptable, easy form to use, and is appropriate for a wide range of subject matter. The flow of lyrical material and stories of narrative poems fit equally happily into its patterns. A fourteen line version of the form is known as a terza rima sonnet.

THE TERZANELLE

This is a hybrid form, a cross between a terza rima and a villanelle. It's one of those forms that seem incredibly complex until you get into the swing of it, and then it falls into place quite simply.

As in both its parent forms, the bulk of the poem is written in tercets. The completed piece is nineteen lines long, and is loosely based on an iambic metre of four or five feet, but many poets find it more effective if it uses line length and metre more freely than would normally be expected in a set form. As in the villanelle, there are fully repeated lines.

There are five tercets linked by chain rhymes, and then a quatrain whose second and third lines repeat the opening line and the middle line of the final tercet in either order. The rhyme pattern is:

A1 B A2   b C B   c D C   d E D   e F E   f A1/F
F/A1 A2

POINT OF CONTACT

When I cannot find my place	A1
within the universe inside my head	B
I reach across and touch your face.	A2
Your warm flesh shocks my fingers. Dread	b
subsides in tangible belief	C
within the universe inside my head.	B
This comfort is my sole relief	c
for torture of unknowing fear	D
subsides in tangible belief	C
when I can look up and see you near.	d
You are the only help I need	E
for torture of unknowing fear.	D
If I am faced with torment, squalor, greed,	e
no depth of pain can swallow me.	F
You are the only help I need.	E
When I forget who I should be,	f
when I cannot find my place,	A1
no depth of pain can swallow me;	F

I reach across and touch your face.   A2

OR

When I forget who I should be,	f
no depth of pain can swallow me;	F
when I cannot find my place	A1
I reach across and touch your face.	A2

SYLLABIC POETRY

One of the qualities that identifies a piece of writing as a poem is a recognisable pattern appearing through it. The pattern may be connected with rhyming words or with metre, but it can be present in a count of syllables. There is a long tradition of syllable count poetry. The Welsh and Japanese languages, for example, have used it for centuries.

The haiku is one of the most famous syllabic forms. The ability to construct a good one has been highly prized in Japanese culture, and was recognised as rather a macho talent. It's a delicate and precise form. Strictly, it consists of just three lines, and has seventeen syllables. The first and third lines have five syllables each, and the second has seven.

The haiku, which is usually untitled, has been described as 'a moment of intense perception.' It encapsulates zen philosophy, and usually has a direct or oblique reference to the seasons, nature, time. It may also invoke a mood.

There are two major divisions of it: the actual haiku - 'an inquiry into the nature of the Universe' - and the senryu - 'an inquiry into the nature of Man.'

Ideally, the first two lines of the haiku open up an idea, and the third offers some comment or additional thought on it. The best haiku are open ended, suggesting that there is more to come.

Pink and white candles
light the chestnut trees, inspire;
scatter confetti.

Because of differences between Japanese and English, many writers believe that the snatch of thought presenting the 'haiku moment' is more important than the precise syllable count. Others stick rigidly to the 5-7-5.

Neither point of view is wrong, but if you are entering your work in a competition, check whether the strict syllable count is to be observed. It's well worth exploring this pattern, which is deceptively simple. It's possible to put seventeen syllables together in a few seconds. It takes a lifetime to master the art of the haiku.

A slightly longer and considerably older version of this form, the tanka, follows the same pattern as the haiku for its first three lines, and then adds another two lines of seven syllables each.

In the tanka, there may be a separation between the third and fourth lines, with the final couplet offering a response to the opening comment.

Imprisoned - a tree
or man or grief as jailer -
manacles still bite.
So Ariel, Caliban
and Ferdinand are all one.

The cinquain was invented in America by the poet Adelaide Crapsey. It has five lines, is unrhymed (as are most syllabic forms), and takes two syllables in the first line, four in the second, six in the third, eight in the fourth and two in the fifth.

As with other forms of syllabic poetry, the pattern can be used as a stanza shape.

ITALIAN EVENING

Twilight
dips sun to quench
its fire where sea ripples,
draws flecks of scarlet, green and gold
down sky.

Across
the bay, shadows
shroud Vesuvius, lights
turn Naples into fairyland,
mist-wrapped.

Bats dart
complicated
figures, chase mosquitoes
through the heat soaked air, flittering
strangeness.

Full dark
is cue to start
artificial brightness,
garish music, clamour to break
the spell.

There are several different forms of the Welsh englyn, where
both a syllable count and a rhyming pattern contribute to the
poem.

Perhaps the easiest to use is the englyn cyrch, which has
four lines of seven syllables each. The first, second and fourth
lines rhyme together. The third line rhymes with one of the three
middle syllables of the fourth.

This form, too, may be untitled.

Yesterday I took your hand   a

as we walked along the sand,		a
begged to know why you must leave.		b
Today I grieve; understand.	b	a

Another attractive Welsh form is the clogyrnach. It may appear with six lines, with eight, eight, five, five, three and three syllables respectively, and using a rhyme scheme:

a a b b b a

Through frosted silence at midnight	a
a single owl hoots, taking flight	a
gliding on ghost wings.	b
Too soon, morning brings	b
lark, thrush; sings	b
for the light.	a

Sometimes the last couplet is merged into one, creating a final fifth line of six syllables. In this case, there is a mid line rhyme, where the third syllable of the last line rhymes with the final sound of the previous two lines. So the example given above would read:

Through frosted silence at midnight		a
a single owl hoots, taking flight		a
gliding on ghost wings.		b
Too soon, morning brings		b
lark, thrush; sings for the light.	b	a

One of the hazards of writing syllable count poetry is that you can become so involved in the cleverness of the arithmetic that you lose something of the poetic quality of the writing; but as with all forms, when you have practised it frequently, the pattern comes more easily and you can stop worrying about the technicalities.

SPATIAL POETRY

Poetry was originally a spoken art. The poet would retain the lore, history and culture of his people in a memorable form, and recite it to entertain and educate. Now that most people can read and have access to the printed word, you can create a form of poetry that relies on its physical appearance on the page for its effectiveness.

There are two forms of spatial poetry, calligrammes and concrete poems, that need to be seen in print to be appreciated. Some of them have little to say when read aloud. The better examples make sense when you hear them; but a dimension is missing if you can *only* hear them, and cannot see how they look on paper.

The use of rhyme and application of metre are optional in these poems.

Calligrammes are constructed as a block of text in a shape on the page. In a positive calligramme, the shape of the text itself reinforces something of the message of the poem. In a negative calligramme, the area/s of white space within a block of text will be the reinforcing agent.

The example at the top of the next page is a positive calligramme, hinting at the shape of the princess' golden ball. Okay, it's a rugby ball - but you get the idea.

The piece beneath it is a concrete poem, which produces an ideogrammic image. The letters and/or words are arranged in a picture compatible with what they are saying. This illustrates how futile it would be to attempt to read the poem aloud; and yet surprisingly, concrete poetry is submitted for radio broadcasting. Strange.

Once there was
a beautiful princess who played
beside a wishing well all day with her golden ball.
The day she dropped the ball, she was inconsolable - until a frog
crawled out of the well, sat slimily on her hand, and spoke to her.
He promised he would get her favourite toy, but only if she said
she would look after him, love him, kiss him. She had to accept.
He made her keep her promise, insisting on the finest food,
demanding his place on her silken pillows, forcing a kiss.
Transformed as a handsome prince, he realised
his inclinations had changed; ignored
the princess; courted her brother.

SNOW


```
    s      s      s              s s  s   s     s    s ss      s      s  s
 n     n        nnn    n     n        n        n     n   n              n
 n        nn
    o     o     o        o    o   o oo          o           o           o
 o
 w     w      w       w        ww     w         w           w           w
 w   ww
 s      s      s s         s       ss            s          sss       s s s
 s     s
 nn    n    n    n       nn       n      n n n          nn          n     n
 n      n
    o o    o          o    o            o         o         o   o     o     o
 o o
```
w settles w drifts w falls ww to w settle dr w ifts w settles ww
drifts w sleeps

THE VALUE OF FORMS

Whether or not you are inspired by the traditional forms of poetry, it's a good idea to practise them and experiment with them. Sometimes the emerging poem itself will dictate the form it ought to take, and it is frustrating to have to put the inspiration on hold while you look up the technicalities.

Writing in set forms is a way of gaining experience in that most vital part of the poetry process - the manipulation of language.

The best way to test the potential of an idea that is not quite working as a poem is to try it out in a variety of forms. Somewhere along the line, the optimum form will present itself, whether in a set pattern or a free verse format. You can always create your own form, known as a nonce form - until you give it a name. As long as you make some rules regarding line length, rhyme and metre - and then stick to your rules - you can join the innovators of set form poetry.

FREE VERSE

Anyone who has never tried it might see free verse as an easy option. After all, you don't have to worry about specific line lengths, rhyme and metre. All you need to do is scrawl a few words across the page, and hey presto! you've written a poem. The trouble is, writing a good free verse poem is a delicate and difficult task.

Even today, many readers will tell you that if it's poetry, it has to rhyme; or if it doesn't rhyme, it has to be prose. As a writer of free verse, you must break down this barrier to communication in order to put your work across. You must make your work utterly convincing as poetry.

Defining the meaning of free verse is difficult. In fact, it is easier to define what is *not* a free verse poem than what is one. Identification has as much to do with instinct and experience of reading poetry as with definition. If your writing puts its message across in a tautly constructed poetic form, and if you can conceive of no other way to convey that message, the chances are it works as a poem.

If you use a set form, a shape is waiting for you. True, you have to mould your message into the shape, and obey the conventions of rhyme positioning and metre. As long as you can do this, you will have produced a functioning poem, or be well on the way to doing so.

Don't forget the important point that with free verse, you are creating the form of the poem while you write. There is no template to guide you – it's being constructed as you go along. So form and content are appearing simultaneously. You have to consider the emerging pattern throughout the writing. For example, if you start a poem with stanzas that are each five lines long and then the final one is only three lines long, the poem 'feels' wrong - unless there is a clear artistic reason for the change.

As with all poetry, free verse springs from knowledge, experience, imagination, emotion or a combination of these. Again, as with all poetry, free verse is a medium for exploring your thoughts, and striving to express something that enthrals you - in an original way. You still need to make sure that this is the best format for the poem you are trying to create. In other words, free verse is one more option, and should be seen as such, rather than used willy nilly. Never forget that there are occasions when a rhymed form is preferable, and other times when you really need a freer pattern.

Free verse lends itself to the application of slant rhyme, but be aware that any use of full rhyme appearing in it will glare at the reader and should be avoided unless it is an integral part of your poem's structure, in which case you may require more than a single use of it. Use as many slant rhymes as you wish, and remember to keep them coming all through the poem, and scattered in the text rather than just at line ends. You've already read that. It's worth repeating.

Word choice in free verse is just as important as it is in rhymed poetry. Don't think you can get away with a less than perfect word or phrase, simply because you are not concerned with full rhyme and metre. Every word you use must be the only word that could possibly fill that space.

Watch your lineation carefully. Resist the temptation to start a new line simply because the current one seems long enough. Use your freedom of line length to 'point' your poem. Let each line's inner tempo contribute to the overall effect. A line consisting of a single word attracts great emphasis to that word. A longer, busy line changes the pace of the poem.

There are occasions when the line ending arises naturally from the sense of your poem. A full stop closing a thought, or a comma suspending one, offers an indication that the line is complete. The difficulty comes when you create an enjambment. This should not break up a phrase awkwardly.

Remember how the shape of your writing will compel the reader's eye to pause for a fraction of a moment at the line end point. Use this to your advantage. Be aware of the tiny emphasis you are creating through this. Try not to squander it by placing an insignificant word such as *a*, *the* or *in* at the end of a line, and completing the idea in the next. Rather, drop the weaker word to start the next line, and end on a stronger one. Natural line breaks make your poem easier to read.

Think about stanza breaks just as you do about line breaks. If the poem is divided into separate stanzas, make sure there is a logical reason for the movement from one to the next. A shift of emphasis or the introduction of a new idea will give you the opportunity to start a fresh stanza.

The final, vital stage in the construction of any poem is its revision. This will be dealt with fully in the next chapter, but suffice it to say that the revision process for a free verse poem is even more stringent than for a rhymed, set form piece.

All this is supposed to demonstrate that the whole business of writing a free verse poem is fraught with problems; but also extremely rewarding. And as with every other aspect of writing poetry, the more you practise, the easier the task will become.

Have a look at this example of a free verse poem and ask yourself three questions:

- Is language used in a way that feels appropriate for poetry?
- Are there plenty of slant rhymes?
- Does the lineation work?

SEA STORIES

I swim,
my body's pressure bruising sea,
pitting its mirror to the crags
that soar, shadowless.
Water whispers ebb and flow secrets,
tells of boats and fish,
of net and wrack,
of tidal surges when the earth heaves.

I slow crawl to a rock
beyond the bay's curve,
clamber out. It absorbs
unsalted water, sucks a dark stain,
holds fragments of my being here
locked in time's memory.

Tales of brine and boulder
cry on gull's wing, grow in coral.

Stirring a rock pool with my toe

startles a crab, whose sideways dart
pulls rays of sun to strike
new angles.

I slither back into the waves,
know breakers and spume
that shock to my presence,
hear mermaids' stories,
insistent song of sirens.

And I am myth, becoming part
of noon's completeness,
melting as each cell reacts
with water, cliffs, and gulls, and sun.

EXERCISES

26 Write a poem on a landscape theme in any form of quatrains.
Now re-write it in at least two other quatrain patterns, eg. ballad
stanza, free verse, rubais. Which is the most effective? Why?
Concentrating on the best version, extend the poem by making
something happen within the landscape.

27 Create a poem in any form about a cuckoo object. This is
simply something that is found where you wouldn't expect to see
it, such as a shoe in a butcher's window, a brightly coloured
feather in your wardrobe, an armchair at a bus stop. Stretch your
imagination to come up with a brilliant 'cuckoo' and an amazing
explanation of it.

28 Write a haiku about air - but including at least one concrete
image.

29 Find some poetry of the past, written at least a century ago. Concentrate on the work of one writer, and study at least four of his/her poems. Now try to imagine just how it felt to be that writer. How was the lifestyle different from yours? What would you have had in common? How must it have felt to have completed those poems? This is an exercise in mind-stretching, but if you are fascinated by it, you might go on to research and then produce a poem about your target writer.

30 What drives you mad? It could be a massive phenomenon or the fact that your train was late. Get even by writing an angry poem about it.

CHAPTER SEVEN

BRINGING IT TOGETHER

Writing a poem sometimes seems like that old circus act where a performer sets spinning plates in motion on bamboo canes and has to dodge from one to the next to keep them all spinning. All the time you are working on the poem, you need to be aware of keeping the preliminary ideas, emerging draft, form, vocabulary choice, rhyme and metre, imagery, grammar and so on spinning through your writing.

Most importantly, you also have to inject it with the X-factor, the indefinable sparkle and magic that will grip your readers.

Maybe the most exciting part of the writing comes when you have reached the end of a first readable draft. At once you have shifted from the *will it come together?* phase into the *end in sight* position. But even though the end's in sight, there is still much work to be done.

There may be complete re-drafts needed, or revisions to the initial draft. You will no doubt find your own 'formula' for addressing this part of the task, but I've offered a checklist below with a few thoughts to start you off.

One thing that really helps with this end part of the process is giving it time. After an initial silent read-through to check it makes sense, and reading aloud to see how it sounds, put your fresh draft away for a few days - preferably a week or more - and resist the temptation to peep.

When you get it out, you will have moved on from the blazing excitement of its arrival and be able to look at it more objectively. That's the time to go through the checklist and confirm that each element on it is working in your poem, and that the whole piece has cohesion.

As soon as you have completed this, put it away again for a while. Repeat the process at a later date ... and again ... and again ...

In fact, you can keep doing this so many times that you can actually revise the life out of your poem. Make sure you hold on to a copy of every stage of your revision. Then when you tell yourself *but I had it right six weeks ago* you will be able to go back to that version instead of tearing your hair out because it's been ripped up or, if you work directly on computer, not saved.

Most poets appreciate that this is the ideal. There are times, though, when you need to hurry the process along, to meet a deadline for submission. If this is the case, and if you're the sort of deadline-keeper who believes that if it's ready ten minutes before the last post goes you've been super-efficient and speedy, there is a way around it.

You can distance yourself from the poem by simply doing and thinking about other things. Write early in the day. Then have breakfast, read the paper and do all the word puzzles. Then you can make an initial revision. Go out for a walk and make sure you speak to a couple of people about anything but poetry. Revise again. Watch a mindless gameshow on TV. Revise again. You get the idea? If you can't put time between revisions, put thought space there instead. Remember, this is the emergency route, not the recommended one.

Even after you have done everything you can to produce a stunning poem, there are times when you need to acknowledge that this one just isn't working. Accepting this fact can be very depressing, especially when you have laboured over your manuscript for weeks. The best attitude to adopt is to remember that the whole business of writing poetry is like studying in an apprenticeship. The only difference is, the apprentice finally qualifies. The poet doesn't - and simply carries on learning.

When a poem has to be set aside as substandard, console yourself with this: nothing can ever take away from you the experience of producing that piece of writing. The fact that you have worked on it and completed it means that the practice was invaluable. So while the individual poem may not have been a success, your writing skills have benefited enormously from the task of creating it.

ANALYSIS OF POETRY CHECKLIST

Whether your revisions are taking place over time or distance, it is helpful to check all of these points. Look at them again each time you work on the poem.

- Do I like/dislike my poem? If I don't like it, will a reader?
- What is its theme? Do I have something to say that is worth saying?
- How effectively is the theme handled?
- Is there originality of subject or approach? Does the work grip or fascinate?
- Could I introduce more layers to make my poem more profound? Would that be a good thing or not?
- What is the form? Does the pattern on the page work?
- Does the form seem appropriate for the poem?
- Are line and stanza breaks appropriate?

- How effective is the poem's vocabulary? Are the words specific or general and abstract?
- Has rhyme (if used) been applied accurately and consistently?
- Has metre (if used) been applied accurately and consistently?
- Has slant rhyme (if used) been applied accurately and consistently? Does it appear at line ends only, or are examples of it used throughout the text?
- Are grammar and punctuation helping the reader or putting up a barrier?
- Are syntax and sentence structuring working?
- What devices of language have I used? How effective are they?
- How good are the images? Are they sufficiently focused and specific?
- Is the balance right, or has one idea been laboured at the expense of others? Are parts of the poem too drawn-out, or too rushed?
- Have feelings and emotions been handled and communicated well?
- Is the general tone of the poem appropriate? Does it speak with the right voice?
- How effectively have I transmitted the thoughts from my mind into the mind of the reader?
- Do I still like/dislike my poem?

Don't forget to streamline this list to suit yourself and your own writing. If you know you have a weakness in a particular area, be extra-probing when you revise that element of your poem. If some of my points don't make sense for you - drop them. See the list as a work-in-progress, and refine it so that it's really helpful for the way you work.

THE POEM'S TITLE

It might seem strange to have talked about so many parts of the writing process without mentioning the bit that the reader sees first. That's because if you begin with a title, it's seldom the best one for that poem. If it helps, have a working 'handle' and then let the poem choose its proper title at the end.

The title is not, however, a mere afterthought. It's a vital part of the writing, and the shop window that tempts the reader in to study your poem. Imagine a reader browsing a book, and running a finger down the list of titles. What will cause the finger to stop? What will intrigue? It's unlikely to be *My Thoughts* or *Musing* or *Autumn* or *Poem* - (maybe the worst title of the lot).

Shakespeare probably takes the cup for the least exciting titles. The sonnets might speak a message of love that resonates through the ages, but it's very difficult to get enthusiastic about *One, Two, Three...* etc.

If you fail to give your poem a name, it becomes known by its first line. This anticipates the opening of the poem, creating an anticlimax. It also makes it very difficult for the speaker who wants to announce a poem, and ends up repeating the announcement as the actual reading commences.

Try not to be too obscure in your choice of title. Even though Keats got away with it, a phrase in a foreign language sounds pretentious.

At the end of the poem, readers should be able to return to the title and say, *yes of course, that was the best title the poem could have*. If they look back at it and say, *I wonder why it's called that? - doesn't fit* ... you got it wrong.

If you can be thinking about the title all the time you are developing, re-drafting, refining and revising your poem, there's a sporting chance that you'll come up with a good one.

Beware of changing the title. If you do, make sure you keep both titles alongside your publication records, or you could find yourself sending the same piece to the same person twice. And yes, that is bitter experience talking.

WHERE TO NEXT?

So you've worked on the poem repeatedly, and you know there is nothing further you can do to make it more compelling. It says what you wanted it to say, and delivers the message with panache. At this stage you can choose from putting it away in a drawer, taking further advice on it, or submitting it. We'll think about the first two options, and save the massive task of submission for the next chapter.

In general, putting the poem away in a drawer deprives it of the oxygen of being aired and read by the world, (or those members of the world who love poetry as much as you do). You've worked on it, honed it to perfection, and then ... nothing. You've got it all dressed up and given it nowhere to go. You've turned it into Miss Havisham, aging in her wedding dress while the cake rots and crumbles and there's no sign of the groom.

There are two occasions, though, when this is the right course of action. One is when the poem was written as a catharsis to help you cope with some inner turmoil or apparently insoluble personal problem, a way of laying a private ghost which you never intended to expose in the public domain. Here, hopefully, the poem has already served its purpose. We should never underestimate the therapeutic value of writing out problems and wounds, but the results are seldom intended for sharing.

Another type of poem that belongs in the drawer is the poem you wrote to vent your anger on somebody – not frivolously but in earnest. If it's your nearest and dearest you risk alienating them for ever if the poem comes to light. If it's your MP or your children's head teacher or the manager of the shop where you got a bad deal, your poem could trigger a lawsuit. On either count, it isn't worth it. Again, the catharsis of writing is enough. Be pleased that you channelled your feelings so constructively, and chalk it down to experience.

You may be wondering what's the point of troubling with all the stages of writing and revising a poem that is going to gather dust in a drawer. There's a very simple answer. You are doing it for yourself, for self satisfaction and personal improvement in your writing. You make your poem as good as it can be, because you deserve the best.

The second option was to take further advice on your poem. This is always a good idea, as long as the advice is sound and comes from a source you respect. The last people who should advise you are your friends and relations. They will either tell you the poem is brilliant because you wrote it, or tell you it's appalling for the same reason. Neither reaction is helpful. So where do you go for proper help?

Most areas have writers' groups, clubs or circles. These vary in terms of the levels of knowledge and experience of their members, but if you find a good one you have hit the jackpot. Many deal with all aspects of creative writing, but some specialise in poetry. A minimal membership fee will gain you access to as much advice, help and experience as you could want.

You will be able to gauge the quality of the group by discovering how many members are published and where, and by the weight of advice you are offered. If you are told that your poem is lovely and you should choose between sending it to a women's magazine letter page and the National Poetry Competition, run a mile. If you get to the end of your reading and there's a moment's silence followed by somebody giving a slight *mmm,* then a couple of suggestions for tweaking your script and the name of the small press magazine you might try it with, you've found the right group.

There are classes in creative writing and poetry all over the country run by adult education centres, U3A groups and private individuals. Many writers have received help beyond measure from dedicated teachers in these establishments. They cost a little more than club membership, but it could be a good investment. If there is a choice in your area, go for the course run by a teacher with a track record of published poetry rather than just academic qualifications. No good creative writing teachers will be offended if you ask where they are published.

If you don't like the idea of regular class meetings but want to get together with other writers, there are day and residential courses you can attend. These cover all aspects of writing, so make sure you book onto a poetry course or you could end up with half a novel - and nobody to tell you there's a hiccup in the metre in the fourth line. A residential course is particularly useful, because you really get to know the tutor and other participants. You have the chance to immerse yourself in poetry without any domestic pressures getting in the way, and you will forge relationships with like-minded people. The cost is, of course, higher when you are staying away from home, but the experience is invaluable.

Many poets meet their first reader on one of these occasions. This is another means of access to a second opinion on your work. A first reader is someone who will look at your poem either when you feel it is finished or when it is still a work in progress, and will offer constructive criticism, help and advice. Although this is only one person's opinion rather than the range of comments you would get from a group, it's coming from somebody who is devoting a lot of thought and attention to your work. The payback is that you do the same for them, giving helpful suggestions for their poems. The bonus is that each person benefits not just from the advice they receive, but also from the in-depth study of someone else's work, so it's a win-win situation.

Some courses also give birth to a postal folio system. A limited number of people - six is a sensible maximum - circulate poems among themselves, and when the folio arrives write comments on the pieces presented. There is a second round for each poem when everyone has commented on it, so that all can see what the others felt about it. When the folio returns again, participants remove the poems that have circulated twice, put the ones with the full list of comments back for everyone to read, and add new ones for comment. Decide on a preferred number of poems to be submitted at one time, (often just two pieces), and stick to your limit of poets. If there are too many people, the advice becomes too diverse and it takes forever to complete each round. The same system can be done by email, saving time and expense; but some poets find it very difficult to read and comment on poems on the screen.

The final outlet for a fresh eye on your writing is to pay for a private critique from an organisation such as the Poetry Society or a writers' correspondence school. You will get a detailed and professional opinion on your work, and can submit questions or problems when you send it in, which your adviser will address. As you never meet, the adviser can give a no-holds-barred opinion on your work without the awkwardness of commenting directly to your face. For most poets, the advice received in this way is of incalculable worth.

EXERCISES

31   Provide yourself with a postcard-sized reproduction of a painting of some narrative subject, such as a battle scene (rather than a still life vase of flowers, portrait, etc.) Study the picture carefully, noting its subject, dominant colours, symbols and the atmosphere it creates. Close your eyes and feel your way into the picture. Become a part of the action. Why are you there? What are you thinking? What happened just before? What will happen next? Write a narrative poem in the first person, using any form. It's even better if you can get to an art gallery to do this, making notes from the original of the picture; but arranging this takes a lot more time and trouble.

32 Start with any word of one or two syllables. Make a list of all the slant rhymes you can find that have sound similarities with your key word. Allow yourself a timed five minutes for this. Now look back over all the vocabulary you have accumulated, and see if there is material for a poem you can write.

33 Take a piece of fruit. Look at it, touch it, smell it. Prepare it for eating, observing every moment of the preparation carefully. Now eat it, sensing texture, taste and smell, even the sound of the crunching, while you do so. That's already very good for you! Make it even better by writing a poem either about the fruit itself, or on any other theme but with a 'backdrop' of the fruit experience.

34 Read all the poems in a small press magazine. Now pretend you are a competition adjudicator, and that these are the entries in the competition. Pick out a first, second and third prizewinner, and justify to yourself your selections and placings. Which poems would you reject at first glance? Why?

35 Write a poem about a bad experience that has never actually happened to you, using feelings and emotions recalled from a bad experience you have undergone.

CHAPTER EIGHT

PUBLICATION

Nothing quite matches the feeling of holding in your hand the book or magazine containing your writing. This is it. You have sent your message winging its way to anyone who will read. Complete strangers will see into your mind. Your writing could influence the way they look at the world. That's power. That's poetry. But before it happens, you need to master the skills of sending your work out.

It is not unheard of for novice writers to bundle up their entire output and send it away to one of the large publishing houses. This leads to the large publishing house returning the entire output. It comes back with a more or less polite note declining the invitation to discover the undiscovered genius.

It is far better to send your work away in small batches to the magazines that are at the heart of publishing new poetry.

The expressions *small press* or *little magazines*, by which they are known, imply something slight and trivial. This is most definitely not the case. The size reference applies to the number of people producing the publication, not to the status of its contents. Many magazines function with a staff of one or two people in sympathy with poetry, and dedicated to bringing the best modern writing to an audience.

There is a wide range of magazines, covering all forms of presentation - from the couple of duplicated sheets stapled together to the glossy paperback book. Within their pages appears the most recent contemporary poetry. It will be vital, experimental, traditional, humorous ... every type of writing is represented.

Some magazines print nothing but poetry, while others include a wide range of features of interest to poets, including editorial comment, correspondence, magazine and competition listings, articles on technique, and reviews of poetry books.

It is unusual to see these magazines in newsagents' or bookshops. Some libraries have them on display, but most people buy them directly by mail order. You will find full details of a huge range of magazines on the web. When you subscribe to one you will hear about others; many magazines carry fliers for other publications, and competition entry forms. You will also learn from these (and from magazines devoted to the interests of writers) about anthologies of poetry to which you can submit material.

Editors would, of course, like you to take out a subscription to their magazines. Without readers they could not continue; but a subscription is not a guarantee of acceptance for your work. Nor will your poetry be rejected merely because you are not a subscriber. You would have to have large quantities of cash to buy all the magazines available, and equally large quantities of time in which to read them. To be realistic, editors accept that nobody can subscribe to everything. It is in your own interests to read as many as you can. Not only will you be keeping in touch with contemporary poetry, you will be learning something of the special interests of each editor.

Do not expect to make a fortune out of your work. You may be paid a few pounds or in free copies of the magazine. Getting your poetry published is wonderfully satisfying, but it is anything but lucrative. Don't be tempted to give up the day job when your first acceptance arrives.

In order to look at the approach to the magazine editor, we'll begin with an examination of how not to do it.

TWENTY WAYS TO IRRITATE AN EDITOR

1 Don't bother to check the magazine. Your poetry is good, and if it's a different style from the sort of thing the editor likes to use, it will bring a pleasant change to the content.

2 Ignore the convention of the covering letter. Just send the poems - the editor knows what they're for.

3 Alternatively, send an effusive covering letter giving a list of your publishing credits, a statement of your views on modern poetry, and a note from your Mum to say how good you are.

4 If you are not sure whether an editor will recognise your talent, try bullying - *If you don't publish my poems I'll cancel my subscription* - or bribing - *I'll recommend you to all my friends if you accept my poems.*

5 Encourage the editor to do some real work by asking for a detailed critique of your submissions.

6 Parcel up your unpublished collected works - all 750 poems - and send them at one time. After all, the editor can simply pick out the best.

7 Hand write your poems. They are so good, the detail about typed work doesn't matter.

8 If you decide to type them, make the work eyecatching by using an unexpected print size like this or like this.

9 Prove your 'green' qualifications by typing four poems onto each side of a single sheet of A4 paper.

10 Don't bother to put your contact details on every sheet - they're on the covering letter.

11 Use pink paper, and see if you can find a suitably eccentric typeface such as this or this or **this**.

12 Centre your work on each page. The computer arranges it, the editor will think it's pretty, and it hides the fact that some lines are much, much longer than others when they're not meant to be.

13 If you can sketch, illustrate your copy with little pictures or stick embellishments onto the ms.

14 Think of all the hungry writers - and editors - who will want to pass off your work as their own. Put the copyright symbol and date on every page.

15 Use really tiny envelopes, as you can still read a sheet of paper despite all the creases.

16 Don't bother sending a stamped addressed envelope (s.a.e.) - just tell the editor to contact you only in the event of an acceptance ... or wait, it's another opportunity to get rid of those fiddly little envelopes.

17 Editors can take ages to get back to you about your work, so why not submit it to half a dozen magazines at the same time?

18 Don't let yourself be messed around. If you have not had a reply within a fortnight, ring the editor just before midnight to find out why.

19 Economise on the time factor by sending a batch of poems to the editor each week for the first three months, and twice a week thereafter.

20 If an editor rejects your work, feel free to point out his/her ignorance and lack of taste, firing off letters and emails to all your poetry contacts telling them to avoid that publication.

Now let's start again, taking each of those points in order.

1 Because there is such a wide range of poetry being published, there are magazines to suit all styles. Although you don't need to take the clinical approach of writing specifically for a market the way a prose writer must, you should be sure to send your work to a magazine whose content demonstrates a preference for your

style. You are far more likely to be accepted if the editor's first impression of your work is *yes, that's just the sort of thing I like.*

2 The covering letter is a courtesy, but ...

3 keep it brief. A simple letter should be addressed to the editor. If the editor is unknown to you, discover and write both names (usually without title) and say something like this:

Dear Jack Daniels

I enclose five poems which I hope you will kindly consider for publication in (magazine title), and the usual s.a.e.

With thanks and good wishes.

Yours sincerely

Only supply additional information if the magazine specifies that it is needed.

4 Any hint of pressure or desperation is a no-no.

5 Editors are fiendishly busy people. It is not their job to give critique, which is time consuming and very hard work. Occasionally an editor will scribble a note on your poem. If this happens, be very thankful - but never expect it.

6 Never send more than six poems at a time, and remember that the editor who accepts your work is only likely to take one or two. Sending too many is self-defeating. You have automatically closed that outlet for all the poems that have been returned from it.

7 Few editors (or competition adjudicators) would consider reading handwritten work. If you have enough faith in yourself to write a poem, you should be sufficiently resourceful to arrange for it to be submitted in print.

8 A plain typeface such as Times New Roman and twelve point print size look appropriately businesslike.

9 Every poem, however short, should be on its own sheet of A4 paper.

10   If you want to be sure the editor knows which are your poems, put your name, address and, if you wish, phone number and email address on every sheet. Editors like to shuffle and sort through poems, and they can easily become separated from your covering letter.

11   Stick to the white paper.   Show the editor you are a professional.

12 Centring is the curse of the computer. There are a few rare poems which need to be centred because of their content. Wherever you can, left justify your work, leaving a good margin. That makes your poetry far easier for the editor to read.

13 See 11.

14 As in all walks of life, most of the people you deal with will be honourable and wouldn't dream of ripping you off.   Of course, there are exceptions, but these are in a tiny minority. It's a sad fact that those writers who safeguard their poems most zealously are the ones least likely to produce anything a discerning editor would want to pinch.

15   C5 envelopes are preferred, so you can fold your poems once. If you are only sending one poem for any reason, the long narrow DL envelope is fine. (A poem folded neatly once tends to be less creased than a poem posted flat in a C4 envelope.) Either C5 or DL takes an ordinary postage stamp rather than the 'large letter' premium one - but do be careful not to use paperclips with a pronounced lip, as these can render the package too thick for standard postage. No editor is likely to stump up the postal penalty for underpayment.

16 If you don't send s.a.e., it looks as if you couldn't care less about the fate of your submission. So you really don't care about your poems.

17 Although there is a case to be made for multiple submissions of full collections, it's regarded as simple bad manners to submit the same batch of poems to two or more editors simultaneously. If you do so and a poem appears in two magazines, the sky won't fall and you won't be tortured on the rack; but you will find that at least two editors are loath to trust you next time.

18 Learn patience. If you haven't had a reply within six months, a gentle nudge - perhaps in the form of a covering letter with another set of poems - is in order.

19 No matter how good you are, no editor is going to want your work in every edition of a magazine. Space out your submissions, never sending more often than the frequency of publication of the magazine. If you find this frustrating, extend the range of magazines to which you submit.

20 Poetry publishing is a small world; and you just might want that editor to consider your writing in the future.

These comments make no mention of online submission to print magazines. Some of these accept emailed poems in attachments, but it's worth checking the publication's requirements before you submit in this way.

It's important to keep records of all your magazine submissions, noting the poems sent out, their destination, the date of sending and the outcome. Apart from helping to keep your life organised, this means you can see at a glance where each poem is, and you will be able to make observations about editorial preferences. It doesn't have to be in a sophisticated filing system. An exercise book or computer file is ideal.

You may have noticed a glaring omission in this talk of sending out your poems, and that's any mention of the explosion in online magazines. This point has been left until the end, because there's no denying that the pleasure of holding that publication with your poem in it far outweighs the joy of seeing it appear on the screen. But the internet offers a huge array of outlets.

The number of online magazines is increasing all the time. Some can be accessed free of charge, while others require a paid subscription. Some also have printed editions, while others are purely online. Titles come and go, so rather than suggesting specific ones I'll recommend looking at a general website, such as that of the Poetry Library at the Southbank Centre, for up-to-date information.

ANTHOLOGY PUBLICATION

There is something especially rewarding about appearing in an anthology. Your work is rubbing shoulders with lots of famous poets, and will reach a much larger readership than it would in a magazine.

Anthologies usually have a theme, which may be subject, time or poet related. So there are anthologies of railway poems, sea poems, ghost poems, love poems, and so on; anthologies of twentieth century poetry, post-9/11 poetry, etc.; and anthologies of poems by women, members of writers' groups, or other specific sets. Many selections cross boundaries. You could have an anthology of war poems published by soldiers who fought together in 1914-1918, for example, satisfying all the categories.

Sometimes an anthology compiler approaches you to ask whether a specific poem can be included in a book. When that happens, it's brilliant. You don't have to do anything except check the copy, sign a permission form and bank the cheque, and a whole new set of readers will see your work.

Often a general appeal goes out to supply poems for a forthcoming anthology. You may find this in a magazine or newsletter, via the internet or on a personal email. (If an anthology compiler likes your work, s/he will be more than happy to add your name to an email list.) Always make sure you submit in good time before the deadline, and remember that everyone else who submits has received the same information about the forthcoming publication as you. Try to find a new angle on the theme, or an approach or gimmick other writers won't have considered, in order to give yourself an advantage.

More frequently you see a new anthology on the shelves, and curse quietly because you could have added something amazing to it. Resolve to be extra-vigilant next time, and make sure the editor has your work to hand when making selections.

You will usually be offered a one-off fee for anthology publication. This varies according to the scale of the project, but a rule of thumb is that it should roughly equate with the cost of a week's groceries for one. If it's a tiny company, you might be on beans on toast, but a large firm producing a glossy book could bring you smoked salmon and caviar. You should also receive a copy of the book, and it's a good idea to include a polite request for this when you return an agreement form if it is not already stipulated.

You may be asked to work without a fee, most commonly when the anthology is being produced to raise funds for a charity. If you agree to work on this basis, you should still get your complimentary copy of the book.

Before we leave anthology inclusion, it's worth referring to an interesting publishing phenomenon that gathered momentum in the 1990s. A number of businesses sprang up publishing large numbers of poems in well presented anthologies, but offered contributors no free copy or realistic payment; only a share of the book's profits or the right to buy copies at a reduced price. Obviously, plenty of contributors would wish to have copies of the book with their poem in, and even if the share of the profit amounted to just a couple of pounds taped to a piece of card, it was an acknowledgment of writing merit.

This is a perfectly legal practice. Nobody was trying to pull the wool over people's eyes. It did not constitute vanity publishing. (More of that later). But the scheme could only work if a lot of writers took part, so that there would be good sales. This led to an acceptance of work which was, frankly, below par according to the standards of many poets. So writers who sent in the best poem ever written could be jostling with grim company in the book. If the company your poem keeps is important to you, take note.

CHILDREN'S ANTHOLOGIES

If you have never had the experience of writing for children, do have a go. It's a wonderful way of encouraging young minds to develop in the belief that poetry is a resource to enrich your life. It's even better for releasing the child within you, getting back at authority, and actually earning some money from your poetry.

Most new children's anthologies are themed, and tend to be divided into poems to enjoy purely for fun, and poems that are learning tools.

In the former category, there are lots of opportunities to write about the fun side of school life, families, pets, fantasy and so on, and to be as irreverent as you like.

The learning poems, in the tradition of the very earliest poetry collected for children, aim to instruct in a memorable way. If the instruction can be entertaining, so much the better. Anthologies in this category have covered different periods of history, all aspects of science, ecology, even mathematics, and they tie in with the demands of the schools' curriculum. Needless to say, the content of the poems must be accurate.

It's important to know the age range you're writing for. Once people are over eighteen it's easy, because they are all lumped together. Before that there are general age divisions of about 4-7, 7-11 and 11-15. Poems should be within the grasp of readers of those ages, but may challenge with vocabulary, images and concepts that really make them think.

If you are not in touch with any young people, spend some time reading recently published books of poetry and prose aimed at different age groups, and watch programmes intended for youngsters on television.

Children love poems with rhyme, rhythm and metre, but are also happy with free verse. In most cases traditional grammar, syntax and punctuation are required, to reinforce the young readers' studies of these.

Good taste should guide you in vocabulary choice and subject matter. But it helps to remember that children in the youngest age division find the word *knickers* hysterical, and you can grip the 7-11s if you can introduce *snot* into a poem.

As with adult anthologies, there are mailing and email lists to inform you of publishers' requirements to which your name can be added at your request. The usual fee and free copy are offered, and there's an extra bonus in that editors of new anthologies may select poems originally written for an anthology on a different theme. For example, I wrote a poem about a wind farm for a school science book, which was then taken for a 'green' anthology; and another for a humour collection for very young children which was reprinted in an anthology based on the sound of words. The only thing nicer than being paid for your poem and seeing it in a book is being paid twice for it and seeing it in two.

PUBLISHING A COLLECTION

When you have had a number of poems published in magazines – I'd recommend a minimum of twelve poems in all, with appearances in at least four different publications or edited websites – you may be starting to think about a solo collection of your work. Like magazines, these vary in size from pamphlets or little chapbooks to full length books, and in quality from the photocopied-and-stapled to leather bound hardbacks. Most poets start small, with first collections of maybe 32 or 40 pages.

The first priority is to decide how you want your book to be published, and then you will follow different routes for different options. The two major routes are commercial publishing, sometimes undertaken by the same people who publish poetry magazines, and self publication; and both have advantages and disadvantages.

Facets of going to a commercial publisher are:

- Somebody knowledgeable about poetry is willing to invest in your work, so you know that the quality of your writing is well up to standard - as does everyone who recognises the publisher's name on the cover.
- It costs you nothing. The publisher bears all the expense.
- Once you have bundled the poems away, and in most cases also provided them in an electronic medium, there is little for you to do until the proofs arrive for word-by-word, comma-by-comma checking.
- You don't have to involve yourself with marketing, although publishers expect you to be reasonably proactive about this. They may want you to give readings, speak on local radio, give press interviews, etc.

But:
- It is very difficult to be accepted by a commercial publisher. Lists are contracting as grants are dropping and costs going up. Most publishers give priority to writers whose work they have brought out in the past.
- You have little say in the overall appearance of the book - although you are usually consulted about the cover.
- You have less control over the timing. As much as two years can elapse between acceptance and publication.
- You may receive little financial reward for your book, but most publishers give you some courtesy copies and will either pay royalties or occasionally give you a batch of copies to sell, from which you keep all the income.

If you decide to follow this route, you will need to put together a proposal package to send to the publisher. This consists of a covering letter, preferably no longer than one page, (to introduce yourself and say a little about where your poems have been published), four or five sample poems, and s.a.e. for reply.

There are different problems if you self publish:

- You will need to be particularly careful about selecting material. There is no editor to tell you if something is not quite up to standard. You can, however, ask someone like your first reader to edit for you, or engage a professional editor. Be sure to include some poems that have already appeared in magazines, and so been subjected to editorial selection processes.
- You will have to cover all costs yourself.
- It is up to you to prepare the ms. fully, or to pay for this to be done. You will need to select a printer.
- You will have to do all your own marketing. This is fine if you give readings and attend workshops and conferences where most sales of poetry titles take place, but could be a problem otherwise.

But:

- You have total control over the book's contents, appearance and timing.
- You retain all profits from the sale of the book.

These last two points are the deciding factor for more and more poets. Poets take delight in seeing through the whole project of producing a collection, getting it out into the marketplace, however small that is, and having total control of - and enhanced earnings from - their book.

If this is the route you are going to follow, it's useful to begin with the 'template' of someone else's book. Find a book that looks and feels like the one you want to see your work in, and take it to a range of printers. They will be able to quote costs for a book in the same format, and show how you could economise on the project without losing too much in the way of quality, and also suggest ways to enhance the book if you are willing to spend a little more.

Repeat this activity in the virtual marketplace to compare the results with those offered by print on demand websites. These are easy to use, and have the advantage of the 'on demand' factor. You do not have to invest in having hundreds of books printed at once and then finding somewhere to store them. You can order a single book, or ten or fifty, and have them with you in a few days.

VANITY PUBLISHING

This is the area of poetry publishing that is better avoided. It survives because poets desperate to see their work in print can be gullible, and believe the blandishments of companies who tell them they have great talent which ought to be brought into the public domain. The problem is, poetry publishing is uneconomic, and so it will be necessary for the writer to support publication by paying something towards it. Of course, the 'something' may well be the whole amount, and will certainly be a lot more than you ever thought possible.

The name of this practice came about because so many poets were willing to be flattered into thinking that their work had merit, and believing that they only had to have it appear in public for the poetry establishment to swoop on it with joyous abandon. In fact, the opposite is the case. The name of a vanity publisher on the book is its kiss of death. It won't be reviewed or appear in libraries, and few people will take the poet seriously.

Most companies were as good as their word, and produced an attractive book. Others were unscrupulous; they took the money and did as little as possible, sometimes even finding a loophole in a contract that freed them from the obligation of actually binding the book.

The big difference between self publishing and vanity publishing is that the former celebrates the writer's ability to recognise and capitalise on his/her talent, while the latter is responsible for the appearance in print of absolutely anything, without thought for merit.

To be fair, there is one situation in which vanity publishing may be the best option. It's a sad fact that many unpublished writers go to their grave with the unfulfilled ambition to see their work in print, and may even ask the family to publish it posthumously. If the family has no knowledge of the world of publishing, this is a nightmare; but a vanity publisher would be able to resolve the situation by bringing out the book to honour a last wish. Then the expense is a small price to pay for the family's peace of mind.

The good news is that vanity publishing does not have the same hold on the population that it once did. Writers seem to be more aware of the state of publishing these days, and of the options available to them. Putting a lot of money into the profits of a vanity press doesn't figure high on the list.

POEMS ON THE NET

This is a difficult area to discuss, as the internet is such a fluid, ever-changing medium. There's no doubt about the fact that some excellent poetry can be found on the web, and that it's a brilliant resource for tracking down a poem you're looking for. There are on-line workshops and outlets that are reputable and helpful. There are plenty more that are better avoided.

As well as the online magazines mentioned above, vast numbers of poems are put onto blogs and websites, and unfortunately that includes a massive quantity of substandard material.

If you want proof of this, put some general term such as *poetry* into a search engine. Alongside a range of reputable sites, you will find enough dross to carpet several libraries. This exercise raises a wry smile from people who know about poetry … but think of the sad situation for all the wannabees out there who believe their poetry is wonderful simply because it's appeared on the internet.

Unfortunately, it is just too easy to put poems into the public domain in this way. It is quick, costs nothing – and one point you should be aware of is that other people besides yourself can put your poems onto the web. This may be done by magazine publishers who also operate on-line, competition organisers who exhibit winners and shortlisted work, and even well-meaning friends.

While it is fine for editors/competition organisers to present your work in this medium, particularly if they have advised you of the possibility that your poems will go onto a website, the friends may be doing you a great disservice. When your poem has appeared on the net, it is, effectively, published. So this appearance of your magnificent poem would stymie it, preventing it from being entered into almost every competition you'll encounter, and compromising its chances of acceptance for a printed magazine.

Should you have any doubts about the quality of work you see on the net, restrict your browsing – and submissions – to sites edited by professionals you know you can trust. This means that somebody who understands about poetry will be assessing the quality of the work, and accepting it as material that attains a certain standard.

It's unfortunate that as soon as a poem enters the public domain it can be taken and used for purposes other than those intended. Maybe if people buy your book, or a magazine with your poem in, they have acquired some right of possession; but it's galling to check the internet and find your work has been ripped off by a stand-up comedian giving a professional performance, a health authority quoting it on their website, and a rather strange fetishist site. And yes, that's bitter experience too; and all concerning the same poem.

To sum up, the internet is bristling with good poetry sites, but groaning under the burden of the rogue ones. It can give the impression that anything found there is 'up for grabs' without any thought of copyright. It's the most amazing resource of our age; but it is not without problems. Use it, of course – but use it with caution, and always be very discerning when you're choosing where to place your writing.

EXERCISES

36 Have a look at the newspaper - national or local, daily or Sunday. Find a good news story and re-create it in the form of a poem. Change the circumstances slightly, and repopulate it with different characters.

37 Turn to the horoscope page of the paper. Read the prediction for your star sign, and write a poem describing how it comes true.

38 Write a very brief poem on any theme without using a pre-selected letter of the alphabet. If you pre-select *j*, *q*, *x* or *z*, you're a wimp. Although you might just write a brilliant poem, this is rather a silly exercise; but it will make you think about and around your choice of vocabulary, and that's rather a useful exercise.

39 Work on a found poem. This is where you come across a passage of prose text which is not intended to be a poem, but is written in a poetic way. You can find it in the text of a magazine or TV advertisement, on the side of a packet of spice, in the directions for assembling a chair. Treat it as you would an initial draft, and play with it, developing and crafting the passage until you tease it into a complete poem.

40 Make up a batch of 4-6 poems and send them to the poetry magazine your market study has indicated may accept them. Plan a strategy for dealing with them if they're rejected. This could involve giving them an extra revision, and having a second outlet

in mind where they might also appeal. Place another strategy for dealing with an acceptance. This could involve chocolate.

CHAPTER NINE

POETRY COMPETITIONS

Poetry competitions are big business. There are plenty around, ranging in scope from a small contest within a writers' group to national and international events offering four-figure prize money. At one time, many poets thought the bubble would burst and that interest in running and entering competitions would decline. This has not happened, and doesn't look likely to happen in the near future.

There's a long tradition of competition among poets, dating from the time when poetry was respectable, paid employment. The bards would organise contests among themselves to refine their craft and to exclude the incompetent. Although the reasons for competing have changed, the tradition continues.

Not everyone in the poetry establishment approves of poets competing, so perhaps we should look at some of the good and bad points of the whole business.

Competitions aim to encourage and assist poets. They bring poetry into the open, heightening public awareness of the craft. A win or an honourable mention gives enormous encouragement. Some competitions produce books of the best entries, and so provide another publication outlet. Most reward the winners with cash prizes. The largest offer instant fame and recognition to the winners - bypassing the traditional route to recognition via regular publication over a number of years.

In addition to this, they enhance the status of the organising society, bringing it publicity and prestige. And many competitions are run in aid of charities, so good causes benefit from the enterprise.

On the negative side, entering regularly without success may be devastating to an inexperienced writer. An already successful writer may be afraid of losing face if s/he enters and does not win. As your work is being judged not merely on its merit but against every other entry, only a few of the pieces submitted gain recognition – a tiny minority. An editor will take any number of successful poems, whereas an adjudicator is looking for just one winner, and maybe second and third placed entries.

Despite the promise of large prizes, the entry fees can add up to a substantial outlay over the months. Entry fees should be regarded as dead money. There is no way you can guarantee the returns from competitions.

It's a good idea to decide on an amount you are willing to spend on entry fees every month, and then stick to it. Keep it within the limit, say, that you would invest in lottery tickets. The big difference between the lottery and a poetry competition is that you can stack the odds in your favour by submitting top quality writing.

It has been suggested that there is a special style of competition poem, which may be over-commercial or bland. I believe this suggestion to be an insult to the adjudicator's intelligence. The competition poem merely has to be brilliant, and you will see the very best of poetry among the prize winners.

There is no magic formula for writing a winning poem. If I knew one, I'd keep it to myself and win all the acclaim and the rewards. But if you like the idea of competing, here are a few tips to help.

- Research the competition. Does it seem to have a regional bias? A poem about the locality may have an advantage, although you must remember that the adjudicator is not necessarily local. Is it in aid of a charity? You might enter a poem touching on the concerns of that cause.

- Only submit the very best work you can produce. Everyone else is sending their best work - yours has to be better. Excellent poems appear in magazines - the crème de la crème win competitions. You can't always produce a brilliant poem to order. When you know you have written one, keep it in a special file for competition entries rather than risk its being published, and therefore excluded from competitions. Then you will have a body of amazing poems to choose from when you are looking for something to enter.

- If the competition is for poems on a set theme, think around it from every angle to stun the judge with your creativity. If a set form is required, make sure you apply it flawlessly.

- Always enter a poem that will remain fixed in the judge's mind. Think of the adjudicator sifting through hundreds of poems. How can you ensure yours will be memorable and stand out from the crowd?

- Research your adjudicators. What sort of poetry do they write? What themes run through their work? Do they seem to prefer free verse or set forms? Be careful not to send in an imitation of one of their poems; you are merely reminding yourself of their preferences through this study – and you are trying to entrance them, not stalk them. It's a good idea to keep a dossier of details about judges, their preferences, prejudices and foibles. The same names crop up repeatedly, so you are likely to encounter them again.

- Avoid telling the adjudicator how to do the job. There is no need to specify on the poem you're entering the form in which it was written or the line length, unless you are specifically asked to do so. You do not need to affix a note explaining how the form works. The judge knows.

- Keep to the rules to save your time, effort and money. Follow online or postal entry requirements to the letter. You cannot expect a competition organiser to take the trouble to correct your entry, nor will a late piece be accepted, however good it might be. If a competition has a limit of 40 lines, the best poem in the world can't win if it has 41. If it should be pronounced the winner, every entrant whose poem was shorter has the right to shout *Foul!* While some organisers demonstrate great integrity and do not cash the payment of entrants whose work has to be excluded, others will keep the money but not submit entries that break the rules to the adjudicator. Don't let them.

- Keep a record of all your entries to aid your memory, and also to make sure you don't send a poem to an adjudicator who was unmoved by the same piece in a previous competition. If it didn't impress the first time, it won't the next.

- Send for a copy of the adjudication report and winning entries, or look them up on the internet, if the competition organisers make them available. You will see what sort of poetry is winning prizes, and be able to add to your dossier of information about adjudicators.

Does the same name crop up time after time in winners' lists? If so, what does that particular writer have that you lack?

- Always approach competitions professionally. Be businesslike in your entries. A win does more for the morale than a dozen acceptances.

OBSERVATIONS FROM THE DARK SIDE

You will often hear poets muttering about competitions, and complaining about biased, ignorant adjudicators who wouldn't know a good poem from a hole in the road. But let's think about it from the adjudicator's point of view.

Judges do not want to condemn the work they read. They are excited by the prospect of finding a wonderful poem, and approach every poem in the hope that it will be a winner. They know from experience, however, that only a small percentage of entries will warrant second and subsequent readings. In a really good competition, as many as 15% of the entries will be re-read. In an average competition, this comes down to 10%, and if the quality of writing is dire, it's reduced to 5%.

As a judge, you are aware of the time and trouble, work and hope that have gone into every entry. You treat the task with respect, and you treat the poems with respect; until they do something that proves they don't deserve it.

It is not necessary for the adjudicator to read every word of every poem. I work on a 'three strikes and you're out' principle. When I reach the third flaw in a poem, I stop reading, secure in the knowledge that there will be plenty of entries exhibiting no flaws at all.

When people hear this, they have been known to rail against the beastly unfairness, and say that poems can pick up to reach a stunning conclusion. Yes, they can; but the winner will be brilliant all through. A poem that starts weakly can never regain the momentum it has lost. Some poems exhibit three flaws before the end of the first line. If there's no title, a misplaced apostrophe and a *thou* in the opening line, there is no point in reading on.

It's frustrating for an adjudicator to find a brilliant poem that lacks its final polish. A single poor choice of rhyme, a typo or weak image can stop a poem from winning. If you have to revise to the nth degree before submitting a poem for publication, you have to work on it still more before submitting to a competition.

Judges are human. That means their final decisions are going to be subjective. It is easy enough to reject any poems containing obvious errors. This filtering is done throughout the adjudication process. But then you get to the end and you have ten brilliant poems from which to choose a first, second and third. They are technically flawless and each demonstrates artistry in its own way. So you award the prizes to the ones that appeal to you the most.

When the placings have been made, there is no room for argument. The only time when it's acceptable to question an adjudicator's decision is if an entry has been found to have broken the rules, such as in the case of a winning poem that has been previously published, where the rules specifically forbid prior publication.

RUNNING A POETRY COMPETITION

If the whole idea of poetry competitions appeals to you, you might decide to organise your own. This isn't generally done by an individual, but is usually arranged by a group in order to promote poetry in general, and/or raise funds for themselves or for some good cause.

Unfortunately you can't guarantee that you will make a profit, and could even make a loss; but here are a few of the points you need to consider if you decide to follow this route.

- You will need a set of rules. The best way to come up with them is to study the rules produced by experienced organisers, and work out which would be useful for you. You will need to think about a closing date, the sort of entries required, ie. whether they are to be themed or open, maximum length of poem permitted, whether you will allow published/broadcast poems or not, prizes, entry fees and how they should be paid, and details of a winners' anthology if you are intending to produce one. You may be surprised by some of the rules organisers set, including *all poems must be written in English*. Believe me, every rule is made because without it there would be an issue.

- You will have to address the question of poet identification. Judges prefer to work anonymously, so it's better if you ask entrants to supply their identity details on a separate sheet, and then you can number the poems and cross reference the number with the appropriate sheet.

- If you are running the competition to aid a charity, you must have that charity's approval before you go ahead.

- You will need to appoint an adjudicator, and negotiate terms such as whether you will send all entries to the judge or whether there will be an initial sifting to filter out the dross, and the date by which results will be determined. A fee is also decided, usually in the form of an agreed payment per poem judged.

- You will have to organise publicity. Most groups produce flyers, usually A5 size, and distribute them as widely as possible via poetry magazines, libraries, personal contact and so on. Many magazines will give a free mention in a competitions listing page. Local newspapers will also give you publicity. Remember to request s.a.e. from anyone who asks for a copy of the rules, or you will have an enormous stationery and postage bill.

- You can get plenty of free publicity on the internet, with a website and by making good use of social media to spread the word. Accepting online entries will maximise the numbers, but you may have the additional trouble and expense of printing out the poems for the adjudicator.

- You will need to get your bank onto your side, possibly by opening an extra account to deal with the entry fees. Many banks go pale and wobbly if you try to pay in a few hundred cheques for a couple of pounds each. Look around for the best deal.

- You will need to be prepared to cope with all the entries as they come in, knowing that there will be an avalanche in the last month before the closing date. You will also have to get in touch with the winners and, as a courtesy, advise anyone who has given you free publicity of the results.

- If you are going to have an official prizegiving, you will need to organise the venue and speaker, and possibly also arrange for light refreshments for the occasion.

- You will need an infinite supply of patience. Even the best of poets and adjudicators can have their senior moments; and these coincide with poetry competition business with alarming regularity. It helps to learn the art of counting to ten.

EXERCISES

41 Put together a collection of information about forthcoming poetry competitions, and check through your competition-quality file to see whether it would make sense to enter. Plan a programme of entries for the next two or three months.

42 Analyse the winning poem in any competition alongside your own revision checklist. Can you see why it was the winner?

43 Start a 'bring out your dead' file. Go through all the half-formed poems in your records that you know are not working properly. Store them in a separate file, and keep adding to the file when another potential poem bites the dust. When you find yourself with available writing time and a dearth of ideas, trawl through the skeletons. You may find inspiration, or even draw a few good passages on connected themes out of the duff poems, and breathe life into them.

44 Look around the house for some random objects. These may be nicknacks, shells you've picked up from the beach, bits that came out of a cracker, and, at the other end of the scale, valuable ornaments or jewellery. The common factor is that you

have kept them around you. Examine the objects themselves and their significance to give you an idea for a poem.

45 Start a poem from the line: *The saint in me* ... or *The fool in me* ... When you return to this exercise, devise some other characters.

CHAPTER TEN

MAKING THE MOST OF YOUR WRITING TIME

No matter how much you enjoy writing poetry, one of the challenges it presents is finding the time to do it. If your life is full, you may take comfort from the fact that you can grab five minutes to jot down an idea before if flits out of your head. But you will still feel the frustration of not being able to settle down to a good long session of writing on a regular basis.

It would be easy to advise you to get up an hour earlier each morning and write then, or go to bed an hour later each night to make time for writing. This is seldom the solution. For a few lucky poets, first or last thing is the ideal time to write. Most of us are not at our best at such hours. Even so, it's worth looking carefully at your weekly routine to see if you can find any slot of time you could use. Perhaps the early or late extra hour would work once a week, even if it wouldn't be practical on a daily basis.

You may be able to find time in your day job. OK, the boss might complain if you log out and take the phone off the hook, but maybe there's time you can recoup from your lunch break. In a talk, U. A. Fanthorpe described how she could manage twenty minute slots between eating lunch and returning to the desk; so she trained herself to be able to work usefully in these little windows.

There may not be time to create a whole poem in such a tight space, but you could use it to type up a handwritten piece, prepare a set of work to submit to a magazine, jot things down in your notebook or journal, check that your records are up to date, do some quick revision or research, try a flow-writing exercise, or something similar. Of course, this means you would need to keep appropriate materials to hand.

It also helps to keep a list of writing activities you can complete in half an hour or less. Selecting an item from a list is much more time-efficient than pondering *what shall I do today?* Tuck the list into a poetry book or magazine. If you can manage nothing else, you can always read a few poems.

The one thing that can cause problems is the length of time it can take for you to get into the swing of your writing. Many poets need to 'write themselves in', and can spend ten minutes staring at a blank sheet of paper or doodling around the corners of it. If you only have a short time to spare, that's a waste.

The secret is to make appointments for your writing, mark them in your day's schedule, and then stick to them as assiduously as if you were keeping a business engagement. Doing this allows you to look forward to your writing time, and for your head to begin preparing for it in advance. If you can pick a task from your list and decide how you're going to begin working on it - maybe even have a few phrases waiting to be set down - before the time period starts, you will use each precious minute more efficiently.

If you can find an hour or two to yourself, you have a much more useful window of time. You will be able to produce a first draft, work on some revisions, research a theme fully, or explore a few ideas in depth.

Every now and then as a special treat you may be able to find a whole day for your writing. This can be far more productive than you might imagine. At the start of the day, you gear yourself up to the tasks ahead - and the impetus keeps you motivated throughout the hours you've allocated.

Some poets find it useful to spend a day like this in company, working with other writers to boost their creativity. For others, it's better to work alone. In either case, it makes sense to plan a timetable for the day - with the proviso that it will be abandoned if the excitement of a piece of writing takes over, and you will be able to devote all the time that's left to that one piece.

If you are working with other writers and everyone wants to come up with some fresh material, you could arrange to get together in someone's house or a general meeting place, and each participant could bring an idea for an exercise to prompt a poem. You can draw lots to decide whose idea will be used first, and if you have not tried them all by the end of the day you can spend the last few minutes dictating the instructions of the untried exercises to the group, so that everyone can have a go at home.

One drawback to working in a group is that you can be distracted by the company. It's not a bad idea to resolve from the start to save personal chat for coffee and lunch breaks, and/or insist on a period of silence while everyone is producing first drafts.

Apart from learning the new exercises, each member of the group benefits from giving and getting instant feedback; and there's usually an air of camaraderie which can be especially stimulating. Also, you are more likely to keep on task if you're in writing company.

If you like the idea of working to exercises, you can easily do the same thing on your own. You can ask another writer or sympathetic friend to set exercises for you, or work through a number of the ones offered in this book, or prepare your own list of them in advance. If you follow this last suggestion, make sure the exercises are prepared and put away somewhere where they can be forgotten for a while before your writing day. Then when you come to them, they will seem fresh and new.

Some writers can keep working on new ideas ad infinitum, while others need to change activities from time to time in order to be most efficient. If you don't know what works best for you - simply try both ways and see. Be willing to be flexible. You may know you are maximising your skills when you fill the day with a variety of activities, then one day you feel the urge to do nothing but concentrate on a single poem for eight hours. Go with it. It's all part of the business of trusting your instinct, and if instinct guides you away from the norm - that's fine.

PLANNING YOUR WRITING DAY

It helps if you can plot a course through your intentions for a full day's writing, and it also helps to set a limit to the time you will spend on each activity. This exerts a hint of pressure to keep you on your toes, and helps to ensure that you won't overdo one aspect to such an extent that you either become sloppy in your work or sicken yourself of it, engendering negative reactions to your total output for the day.

If you're working in a group, you will need to allow 20 or 30 minutes for the explanation of the exercise and the actual writing, followed by about five minutes per person to read the work out and for initial comments. It isn't worth critiquing in depth at this stage. The poem is too embryonic for detailed criticism. In order to provide some brain-rest between writing exercises, you can build in periods of time for discussion, information sharing or reflection, then go on to the next exercise. Allow 45 minutes for a snack lunch. It's quite useful if each poet brings a little picnic, then the host has to do nothing more than prepare drinks.

As poets work at different speeds, you might like to give everyone instructions for an extra exercise at the outset, which can be accomplished in bitesize chunks. Then everyone has something to work at, and nobody will be sitting twiddling their thumbs while the rest of the group catches up.

Here are a few ideas for the speaking periods between exercises.

Discuss:

- Rhymed poetry has more appeal than free verse.
- What's the difference between light poetry and slight poetry?
- The days of the book are numbered.
- There's no need for a poet to study writing from more than 50 years ago.
- How important is the poem's title?

Share Information by prior arrangement:

- Everyone brings a small press magazine for a spot of 'show and tell.'
- Everyone brings news of a forthcoming competition.
- Everyone brings a quote from another poet about the craft of writing.
- Everyone brings a potted biography (max. 300 words) of a famous poet - living or dead.
- Everyone brings information about a course or other study experience that's been advertised.

Reflect:

- How much of your own life and experience goes into your poetry?
- What was the poem that first captivated you?
- Where was your first publication, and how did it make you feel?
- Which poem are you most pleased to have written?
- How do your family and friends react to your poetry?

This is a very simple timetable for a get-together of six writers. Use it as a template, and tweak the bits you want to alter.

9.45   Meet and greet, ready for a 10 am start. Determine the order of exercises. Set the ongoing task to be worked when you have a few spare minutes. For example, you might give everyone a list of eight stations on a particular railway line, and request a cameo poem for each stop to create a journey mini-sequence.

10.00   First exercise to be described by the person who came up with the idea. (All exercises will be written in 20 minutes with a 5 minute reading time per person.)

10.50   Coffee and discussion: must today's poets be computer literate?

11.15   Second exercise.

12.05   Share information: everyone mentions a poetry connection, such as a poet's birthplace or the scene of a poem, within 40 miles of the venue.

12.20   Third exercise.

1.10   Lunch break.

1.55   Fourth exercise.

2.45   Reflection: the poet whose work has helped me the most.

3.00   Fifth exercise.

3.50   Tea and share results of the journey mini-sequence challenge.

4.15   Sixth exercise.

5.05   Comments and ideas on the day ... and possibly plans for a repeat experience.

5.15   End.

If you're planning to work on your own for a day of exercises, the timetable is much simpler. You may wish to allocate - say - 30 minutes for each exercise, and build in refreshment breaks. You will have time to complete more work. Instead of readings of drafts and discussion periods, you may like to spend a few minutes with the newspaper or listen to the radio for a short while; anything that will give you a brief break from your writing.

Then you'll be fresher when you come to the next task. Your timetable could run:

10.00	First exercise.
10.30	Newspaper time.
10.45	Second exercise.
11.15	Coffee.
11.30	Third exercise.
12.00	Crossword.
12.15	Fourth exercise.
12.45	Lunch.
1.30	Fifth exercise.
2.00	Finish crossword!
2.15	Sixth exercise.
2.45	Listen to a radio music station.
3.00	Seventh exercise.
3.30	Tea.
3.45	Eighth exercise.
4.15	Knit / play with cat / 'phone a friend etc.
4.30	Ninth exercise.
5.00	End.

If you're planning to spend a day on varied poetry activities rather than solely producing draft poems, try the following timetable as the basic template. You'll notice that there are not the same diversion opportunities through the day. Hopefully the range of tasks suggested between the writing exercises will keep your mind refreshed.

The first element of the day provides a list of options that could be used on future occasions. Think up new challenges for the other elements, which you can address next time you plan a varied activity day.

10.00 Read some poetry. You may go through the latest edition of a magazine, dip into an anthology or collection, or theme your reading. If you go for a theme, it could be subject-based, such as autobiographical poetry, narratives, pastoral poetry, humour, etc. or poet-based, such as Victorian poets, Shakespeare's sonnets, poems by living writers, and so on.

10.30   Writing.   Produce a flow-writing exercise on a theme selected at random.   Repeat the flow-writing until an idea emerges for a poem. Write the first draft.

11.15   Coffee.

11.30   Administration.   Prepare a balance sheet for the finances in your poetry life.   What have you spent?   What have you earned?   If the answer is too depressing, prepare a balance sheet for the emotions in your poetry life.   Is this a more cheerful prospect or not?

12.15   Fun.   Put a joke into poetry. Begin with any simple joke, such as the childhood favourite: *Why do elephants paint the soles of their feet yellow? So they can hide upside down in a bowl of custard.* Now render it in the form of a verse.

1.00   Lunch.

1.45   Workshop.   Look in depth at an aspect of technique, and apply it to some poems you have already finished writing. Consider the importance of pruning, for example; cutting every non-essential word and phrase, paying particular attention to little words such as articles and conjunctions, and to adjectives, adverbs and unscheduled repetition.

2.30   Form.   Explore the dynamics of a form you haven't tried before.   There are a few examples in this book, and hundreds more in poetry textbooks and on the internet.

3.15   Tea.

3.30   Forward planning.   Make a list of ten ideas for poems you would like to write in the future. This period also gives you an opportunity to plan your next writing day, or think up some new exercises to try.

4.15   Writing.   Open a book and, without looking, put your finger down on five different words. Draft a poem that includes all of the words.

5.00   End.

CAUTION

In a chapter that encourages poets to make the most of their writing time, this caveat may seem unnecessary and wilful; but it's an important consideration.

Poetry has a way of expanding to fill all the time available - and then some. You can become so involved in it that it takes over your whole life. If your life involves other people, remember that there are times when you have to put poetry back in its box and tell it to behave or you could find friendships and relationships damaged because of the time you spend on it. If your nearest and dearest are also poets, show them this paragraph too. And accept my sympathy.

There are two other reasons for turning your back on it occasionally. There are times when you need to allow your mind to lie fallow, to rest from writing so that you can re-group your mental and emotional resources and come back refreshed and raring to go. There are also times when you need to descend from the ivory tower and rub up against the real world. That is what provides the content for your poems, and injects them with life and with passion.

EXERCISES

46 Write a poem in any form from the viewpoint of a supernatural being - a vampire, unicorn, dragon, sea monster or similar.

47 Make lists of four 10-minute poetry activities, four 20-minute ones, four 30-minute ones and four 45-minute ones. When you next have some free time, try out one of the activities on a timed basis, and note whether it takes the allocation you had planned, or is completed more quickly or more slowly. Repeat the

exercise when you have free time within the other suggested limits. You'll achieve the tasks, and also get an idea of how well you can gauge your pace of work.

48 Write a poem about any sport you practise, follow or loathe.

49 Prepare a themed alphabet you can write up as a poem for adults or children, eg. a children's alphabet could be of names: *My friend Alice* ...... *My friend Ben* .... *My friend Chris* .... followed by rhyming, rhythmical phrases.

50 Create a frame with your index fingers and thumbs. They may be just in contact or overlapped, and should be at arm's length. Write in powerful, specific detail about something you can see through this frame. Mould your writing into a poem.

CHAPTER ELEVEN

LET'S TALK ABOUT IT

As a poet, you have two fascinating sources for performances you can deliver. You can read your poems in public, giving you the amazing experience of watching audience reaction to your writing; or you can give a talk about poetry - which could be based on your own experiences or information of interest about the craft and its practitioners. For either, there's some important preparation to be done. We'll start by looking at giving a reading.

Most poems work in two dimensions. They can be enjoyed when read silently from the page and when heard spoken aloud. Exploring the techniques of speaking poetry enables you to put your writing across to best advantage. A good poem is enhanced by a competent reading, and elevated by an inspired one. A bad poem can be made to sound tolerable if it is read well enough. Poor reading converts the most inspiring poetry into dross.

The advice given below is aimed primarily at speakers who are reading to an audience; but remember that employing these techniques will make the whole business of reading poetry a more pleasurable experience, even if you are speaking aloud just for your own amusement.

If you wish to undertake a serious study of poetry-speaking techniques, you need the assistance of a qualified and experienced teacher of elocution (nowadays more likely designated 'speech and drama'). But if you require just a little guidance on the subject, these thoughts may help.

BASIC PREPARATION

Before you begin to start thinking about the speaking itself, it's important to consider your stance and breathing. The posture should be relaxed but controlled. Stand straight, with your weight evenly balanced over both feet, and feet a few inches apart. Resist the temptation to raise your shoulders as you breathe in. Try not to incline your head up or down, creating tension in the neck. Be prepared to take in the entire audience - close and distant, left and right - rather than targeting one or two people directly in front of you, and speaking straight to them.

If you are reciting, let your hands drop loosely at your sides. If holding a book, make sure that it does not obscure an audience's view of your face, depriving the listeners of an extra dimension of communication through facial expression. You may have decided to use gesture to enhance your performance. Make all movements definite ones; fluttery hands make the audience nervous. (Fiddling with clothing or jewellery, or jingling coins in a pocket, has a similar effect). Should you be sitting down to perform, sit straight (rather than slouching) to aid breath control. Again, make sure that you are in control of your hands. Clenching them, wafting them around ineffectually or repeatedly touching the chair will make you look anxious and will unsettle your audience.

Breathe from the diaphragm, to maximise your lung capacity. Before you read, a few very deep breaths taking air in and out through your nose will fill your lungs and also help to relax you. (While actually speaking, it is better to breathe in through the mouth, as this is a quicker and quieter process.) If you have some privacy, sing a long, loud humming note as you exhale to aid resonance. Do this five or six times. Then produce a few loud, sustained 'aaah' sounds, throwing the sound forward. This will help to warm up your voice and enable you to project the sound so that everyone in the audience will hear.

INTERPRETATION

As you know from the writing of it, a poem is taut and compact, and each individual word is a vital part of the organic whole. Every nuance of vocal expression that can be included to aid the communication should be used, but applied with delicacy, not overdone. Don't ignore the natural cadences of language. Normal pronunciation produces a flow of stressed and unstressed syllables that give language its rhythm. Be careful to avoid robotic delivery, which occurs when you put the same weight of stress onto every syllable.

The words you selected for the poem offer the best indication as to how they should be spoken. To take an extreme example, it would not be logical to shout *murmuring* in your loudest voice, nor would you try to impose a staccato delivery on a phrase like *sleep too deep for dreams*. Make the most of the onomatopoeic quality of words, so that you enhance their meaning by speaking them out in a tone compatible with that meaning.

A well modulated voice is the best vehicle for a spoken poem. Modulation, or variety in delivery, works in a number of dimensions:

- The pitch of the voice - high and low notes - can be varied to combat the boring effect of speaking on a monotone. Within pitch, subtle movement or inflection adds pleasing shades of colour.

- The speed of delivery can be adjusted, giving, for example, a fast, vigorous pace to an action-packed passage and a more languorous quality to a reflective piece. As a general rule, however, speech should be slower than you expect. We all tend to speak quickly when treating familiar subjects; and the poem you are speaking is very familiar - to you. The audience needs time to absorb the words and the message they are conveying. You should never speak so quickly that the listeners cannot keep up with you.

- Connected with the rate of delivery is the use of pause. Pausing makes sense of the phrases from which the poem is constructed, and allows the audience to 'catch up' with what you are saying. A pause can arise from the grammar of the poem, indicate punctuation, or merely aid the sense of your reading. Pausing can also help to retain the shape of the poem. Stanza breaks can be indicated by fairly long pauses. The tiniest pause - a mere suspension of the sound - can demonstrate the structure of lines and positioning of line breaks by indicating an enjambment, ensuring that the sense at the end of an unpunctuated line runs into the next line. This indication of the structuring of the poem is particularly useful for free verse, where line and stanza ends are not dictated by rhyme or metre.

- Like pace, volume can be varied to reinforce the message of the words. It is essential that the poem should be heard throughout the room, and you will probably have to speak more loudly than you would in ordinary conversation to achieve this - if only out of consideration for the size of the area in which you are performing. An inaudible delivery defeats its own object. But within the limits of audibility there is a broad range of acceptable levels. If you are speaking in a hall with a microphone, use it. It is there because the size or acoustics of the room demand it, and is essential for people using hearing aids. Unless it's the sort that's attached to your clothing, it should be placed a few inches away from the mouth and slightly to one side, (usually just to your right). If it is fixed to a stand, try not to move your head about too much. You don't have to work so hard for projection if a microphone is used; clear, conversational levels of speech are ideal.

- Consider your tone quality - harsh or gentle, hectoring or lyrical. Try saying a simple sentence, such as *I wish you wouldn't do that*, with a range of intonations. How would you change your tone if saying that sentence to a small child, an employer, a partner, a good friend, your dog? All of those tonal variations - and dozens of others - are available to help you to animate your delivery.

It's impossible to offer a blueprint to be followed slavishly when devising the best manner of speaking any given poem. Each poem is a separate case, and each will need to be studied and considered in a different way when you shed the poet's hat and put on the speaker's.

With practice, application of the techniques of verse speaking becomes instinctive; but remember that it is as important to work on your delivery as it is to craft the poem in the first place. Above all, make sure you are convinced that your delivery of a poem will bring its words to life for your audience.

CHOOSING YOUR PROGRAMME

Think carefully about the people who've come out - possibly on a cold winter night when TV and a glass of red beckoned - and remember that it's your job to give them a brilliant time. You have worked on your delivery of a range of poems. Now comes the all-important question of which you're going to perform. There are four major factors in making this decision.

1 Timing. If you are 'testing the water' by reading some of your poems in an open mic session, you must be aware of all the other people planning to read. If you exceed your time allocation by only a minute, you will cause annoyance and frustration to the other performers. As they will represent a good proportion of the audience, this is to be avoided. So if you have just five minutes to play with, make sure you have practised your reading and know that you will be able to complete it in four minutes fifty seconds. Remember to include introduction time, if you plan to say anything in addition to the actual poems. Should you be giving a longer reading, timing's equally important. Speak for too long, and your audience will start to get restless. Finish too soon, and they'll feel short-changed. Always prepare more content than you think you will need, and be willing to drop a few poems if you're right. Make sure you don't drop the most spectacular ones, which should launch and close your reading.

2 Balance. Aim to provide a variety of readings unless you have been invited for one specific purpose, such as to launch a new collection. By including poems on all sorts of different themes, free verse and set forms, serious and comic pieces, and by planning the order of readings to give an easy flow from one poem to the next, you will produce a balanced selection.

3 Audience. Be sensitive to 'difficult' areas. If you're giving a reading in a residential home for elderly people, your hilarious poem about dementia may not be appreciated. If your audience is the local civic society, keep the 'I hate this town' poem under wraps. This is not about compromising your individuality - it's about good manners.

4 Occasion. Nothing pleases an audience more than to hear a poem written especially for them and for the occasion the

reading marks. If you've been asked to read a few poems at a wedding, make sure there's one about the happy couple. If you're reading at a city's literature festival, include one about literary figures who hail from that place. All this may seem like a lot of unnecessary stress. It's quite easy to keep a few poem templates around, and tweak them to suit the individual occasion; and it will get you lots of brownie points with audience and organisers.

GIVING THE PERFORMANCE

Unless it's a very brief open mic situation, always begin a reading or talk with some complimentary remarks - a *thank you* for the invitation, a comment about an attractive venue, an acknowledgment of a gracious introduction. This is not just polite, it's a way of getting the audience on side. Likewise, a *thank you* to a generous audience is a courtesy just before you leave the platform.

There is no substitute for thorough rehearsal of your reading. Always practise a reading - or a talk - aloud. It invariably sounds perfect in your head. Practise until you can - almost - recite your poems in your sleep. This rehearsal, however, has a paradoxical side. The more you rehearse, the more you should strive for a spontaneous performance. Make the audience think that you are saying a poem perfectly after no more preparation than a brief glance, and you have achieved speaking success. If the listeners believe you have learned the piece by rote and chanted it parrot-fashion, they will not be impressed.

You will need to decide whether to introduce your poems or just to give their titles. I like an introduction. It gives the audience something more than they can get by just buying your book and reading the poems, which would almost negate your performance. Just be careful, though, that you don't give the poem away in the introduction. You could add snippets such as: *This is the first poem I had published* or *I wrote this poem in five different forms before I settled on this one* or *Have you ever moved house? If so, you'll understand why this is as much a horror story as a poem. We moved ten years ago, and I've still got the scars ...*

If you are speaking to a group of writers, a little technical information is appreciated; but you have to strike the balance between being informative and insulting their intelligence. A 'we're all in this together' approach can be helpful. You can say things like: *Isn't it tiresome when you're writing a villanelle, you get all the rhymes and repeats in the right places, and then you can't structure a final sentence at the end of that last quatrain?* You have given all the information people need to appreciate the form on a heard level - but without suggesting they might not have known it before.

If you are reading the poems, try not to keep your eyes fixed to the page. Look up frequently, showing the audience that you are communicating the poem to each individual. Pay particular attention to places where you will need to turn over, to ensure that it is done smoothly and without any pause.

Make sure you have a clear list of page numbers, or use book marks to avoid fumbling and delays that will evaporate the mood your reading has created. Post-it notes are ideal, or you can make a multi-bookmark by cutting up to about eight lengths of narrow ribbon to 40-45 cms., then tying them together with a knot at one end. Each strand is a separate bookmark, and of course you can colour code them if you wish. As you read the poem, you simply put its strand over the outside of the book, and you can hold it in place. If you're reading unpublished poetry, place your poems in reading order in the transparent pockets of a presentation display book. Use A5 rather than A4 to be more audience-friendly.

If you have memorised the work, arrange for someone to be available to prompt you if necessary. Hopefully you will not need this service, but it gives you a lot more confidence to know it's there.

Be aware of your physical appearance on the platform. An uncluttered look will keep the audience's attention focussed on the words you are saying. Bizarre attire draws it away from the content.

We have already looked at ways of using the voice to reinforce the message of the poem, but try to avoid any affectation in your speech. Some people have a 'poetry voice' like a telephone voice, and the change of tone from conversational to poetic sounds absurd. I've heard an excellent poet killing every piece in delivery by adopting an unnaturally high pitch and elongating all the vowel sounds.

A regional accent is appealing as long as it is authentic. Use your natural Liverpool or Cornish or Geordie accent with pride, but don't try to adopt a dialect that doesn't come naturally to you unless you have great expertise in this area.

Some readers don't just deliver a quality reading in a true voice, but like to perform with exaggerated voice work, movement and gesture. This overacting can be exciting occasionally, but quickly becomes tedious if a lengthy performance is delivered in this way.

Unfortunately in many cases such exaggeration is affected in order to mask the fact that the poetry being performed is weak or inadequate. The better the poetry, the less 'hamming up' is required.

Remember, though, that there are exceptions to this point. Some stunning poems are produced with the sole intention of being performed, not read from the page. The street rhythms and intensity of rap and hiphop work wonderfully when delivered to their beat, but were not intended to be read in silence.

Always speak with total sincerity. Believe in your poem and in your delivery of it. Then the integrity of your performance will bring your words to life for the audience, who will relish and identify with them.

GIVING A TALK

The other performance outlet for a poet is to give a talk about some aspect of poetry. Just as with a reading, this must be carefully planned and rehearsed. If you've read the advice about giving a reading, remember that most of it also applies when you're giving a talk.

An autobiographical talk is probably the easiest to do, because it doesn't really involve research, only recall. Try to make it as lively as possible. Beginning with *I was born in the early hours of a Thursday morning* signposts a boring evening for the audience, unless it is speedily followed by a funny anecdote, coincidence or other point of interest. Remember that you're giving the talk because you are a poet. Spending the first ten minutes talking about learning to walk and attending primary school will not excite. Speaking about the first poems you studied at school and how you felt the first time you tried to write one will be far more interesting.

Plan your talk with a logical route through the material. Most autobiographical talks are chronological. If this is the case with yours, don't see it as: first decade, second decade, etc. Instead, think in terms of: studying English at university, editing a magazine, seeing my first collection in print, and so on.

Demonstrate to the audience that you have plotted the route with care. Keep them informed of where you're up to, and they will feel safe and confident, secure in the knowledge that you know what you're doing. If you start the talk by saying something like: *I thought you might be interested to hear how I became a poet, the difference it's made to my life, where I am now, and what I'll be doing next* then you can go on to say things like: *well, so much for the difference poetry has made in my life. Now I'll move on to the current situation ...* That way you will have reinforced the message that you are leading the audience competently and confidently.

Make brief notes as a prompt in case it's needed. One side of a postcard should be big enough for the notes for a half hour talk; after all, it is only a prompt. Nothing depresses an audience more than sheaves of A4 from which you read, or 97 cue cards you turn over and drop.

Never forget that your prime duty is to entertain the audience. They'll have far more sympathy with you if you can make them laugh than if you regale them with harrowing tales of your hard life. At all costs, avoid bragging to them. Be a little self-deprecating - not enough to be tiresome, but sufficiently to appear modest. Be prepared to laugh at yourself. A funny story told against yourself is hilarious. A funny story told against somebody else is embarrassing.

Even when you are giving a talk rather than a reading, feel free to add a couple of your own poems. These will illustrate points you're making, give a change of tempo which is as appealing to the audience as it is to the speaker, and may encourage the group to ask you back to read some more. This is an advantage poets have over other writers. Because a poem is short and complete in itself, you can add a few examples without risking the onset of boredom.

Of course, you don't have to talk about yourself. You can craft a talk about a poet who fascinates you, the history of poetry, developments in children's poetry, how poets came to write best-loved poems ... anything. Make sure your facts are accurate. You can guarantee that a talk about Tennyson will attract people who know more about him than you do. Don't let them catch you out. If you are preparing a new talk and need to research the subject, expect to spend half an hour on research for every minute of delivery.

Here, too, you are setting out to entertain an audience. Interesting little factoids, anecdotes and witty asides will help. Make sure you have plenty to include, and remember that the best off-the-cuff remarks are the ones you prepared earlier.

In any style of talk, timing is as important as it is in a reading. It's a good idea to have different versions of your talks, so that you can give 30, 40, 50 or 60 minute versions of the same thing. Just make sure you know which the audience requires before you go to deliver it.

A final thought about delivering the talk. Enjoy it. Remember, the audience is on your side. They want you to speak well, and they want to enjoy what you say. Your enjoyment is infectious.

QUESTION TIME

There are some frequently asked questions for which you can be prepared. It's useful to have an answer ready for each of these:

- Who's your favourite poet?
- How long does it take to write a poem?
- How do you set about the actual work of writing?
- If it doesn't rhyme, how do you know it's a poem?
- I've always wanted to write poetry. How do I start? (A million extra brownie points if you tell them to buy this book).
- Why do I keep getting rejected?
- Do editors favour known names?
- What does a poet earn? (Most adults are too polite to ask this, but give readings in schools and you'll hear it all the time).

Whenever you come up with a brilliant answer to a question, make a note of it while it's still fresh in your mind. It's bound to come up again.

Don't be embarrassed to say you can't answer a question. If someone tries to floor you with *What's the set form for an epithalamium?* and you're not sure, don't waffle and guess, but ask them to give you their contact details at the end and get back to them with the information. (There isn't a set form, it's just a poem to commemorate a wedding). If you're really stuck, suggest they Google it.

MAKING THE PLANS

Everything you have read in this chapter so far is dependent on your having an engagement to go to. There's a fair bit of hit-and-miss in the business of getting bookings. The important thing is to let people know you're out there and willing to speak. You can do this in a number of ways.

- Take advantage of every networking opportunity. Whenever you get together with other writers or groups who need speakers, carry business cards, leaflets or brochures you can leave with them.
- Check whether your reference library keeps a register of speakers.
- Publicise your talks on your website.
- See if you can find an angle to interest your local paper or radio station. If you can tie in your publicity with the publication of your new collection of poetry, you can kill two birds with a rather glittering stone.
- Advise your council's arts department of your venture.
- Scour the local press for accounts of groups that welcome guest speakers, such as luncheon clubs and social groups. Approach the secretary with your details.

These are all means of getting bookings without any cost to yourself, other than the provision of business stationery - and if you shop around you will be able to supply that for minimal costs. If you wanted to go a stage further and invest in the project, you could contact writers' groups individually with a package of information and leaflets.

When a speaker organiser gets in touch with you, make sure you get all the information you need. This includes:

- The name of the group inviting you, expected size of audience, layout of the room and whether you will be using a microphone.
- The nature and duration of your presentation. If you offer a range of talks, make sure you know which is required. If you go intending to speak for 40 minutes on *Shakespeare's Life and Loves*, it's difficult to switch to an hour of readings from your own work - even supposing you have the material with you.
- Check whether you will have an opportunity to sell your books, which can bring greater rewards than the talk itself.
- The date, time and venue of the talk, along with instructions for getting there and parking arrangements when you arrive. If you are travelling by train, check the availability of taxis and time it will take from the station to the venue, or ask whether someone could give you a lift.
- Contact details of the organiser, preferably including a mobile number. If you're delayed by a traffic jam when you're only a mile from the venue, chances are the organiser will already be there so the home number is useless.
- If your presentation demands a flipchart or powerpoint, check that appropriate provision has been made.
- If you'll be a long distance from home, ensure that you will be provided with accommodation, which may be bed and breakfast or a stay with a group member. Decide for yourself whether you can reasonably get home. (I don't drive further than 75 miles after giving a talk).
- Confirm your fee. This is always the dodgy part. It's not unreasonable to expect to be paid the same for your talk

as you would pay anyone else for trade or professional services; but if your audience is six octogenarians in the vicar's vestry, you may need to compromise. I ask for 'your usual fee' plus travelling expenses. If you do this, most people deal with you fairly, and some generously. Be prepared, though, for a group to admit that they don't pay fees, but give you a memento of the visit. From experience, this can be a bouquet of flowers (beware dahlias - I left a bunch heaving with earwigs on a train once), a box of chocolates, or a 'dayglo' orange knitted poodle to be fitted over a spare lavatory roll. Yes, it's unprofessional and I really should hold out for the sort of money I'd pay the plumber; but it's fun to do, you get to meet some wonderful people, and as long as I'm making something from the occasion, I don't complain. Well, not too loudly. Incidentally, sometimes you're asked to speak for a charity. If that's the case I waive the fee but expect my travelling expenses, unless the cause is especially dear to my heart.

It's a good idea to contact the organiser by phone or email shortly before you are due to give your talk. Confirm all the arrangements, and give an idea of your estimated time of arrival. Check who'll be meeting you and where. Be positive and confident. Everyone is going to have a lovely time - and you'll make sure it happens.

EXERCISES

51   Have you ever wondered how it would feel to have a diffcrent name? Starting with *If I were* - and adding the name of your choice, list the aspects ot life that the named character would have, eg. *If I were Dolores I would drive a sports car/ be slim/ train to be a manicurist.* Next, add a phrase to comment on or explain

each, or to add a touch of humour or pathos. You will have the start of a free verse list poem, and only need to add a punchline to finish the draft.

52 Write an upbeat poem on a cheerful theme. It's much harder than writing something depressing.

53 Plan an open mic style reading of your poetry, with three poems and apt introductions. Practise the reading, and time yourself.

54 Make a list of words that fascinate you. They don't need to work together, but have been chosen just for their sounds. Say them aloud repeatedly, rolling the sounds around your mouth. Now select a couple of the words to start a flow-writing exercise.

55 Look in the TV paper at the names of programmes. Use one as the title of a poem. Picking the name of a programme you have never watched gives you a better chance of producing something original. While revising, you can change the title if you wish.

CHAPTER TWELVE

ENJOY

One advantage of poetry over other forms of writing is the fact that you can have fun with it. While it's incredible to hold a book or magazine containing your work, and to see the response of the audience when you're giving a reading, there are other uses for poetry that are purely for pleasure. Why not indulge yourself and try a few?

Assemble some poems about a specific period in your life, or a holiday you've enjoyed, and mount them in a pocket-sized photograph album with appropriate pictures, postcards or tiny mementoes to create a mini-memoir.

Write seasonal poems to stick inside your Christmas cards, rather than having to write letters to everyone or prepare a catch-all round robin letter.

If you're sufficiently extrovert, create a verse monologue to deliver at a party or family gathering. You can make this interactive by including a refrain everyone can say together.

If you want to bring poetry to an occasion but don't like the thought of standing up and delivering it, leave pens and paper lying around with an invitation to write a specific type of poem, such as a limerick. Then you can ask everyone to read their work out to the assembled company.

Make a poetry calendar, with a new poem and illustration for each month of the year. You can buy the blanks for doing this yourself, take it to a printer, or prepare the calendar on the internet.

You may already be producing occasional poetry, written for someone's special celebration, such as a 'big' birthday, retirement, or on the birth of a baby. With a little imagination and a trip to a good crafts shop, you can produce copies of your poems in different settings, both for your own pleasure and to make original gifts.

If you are good at calligraphy, use this skill to make the copy of your poem. If not, all you need is a computer. Even the most basic machines have a range of fonts in plain and ornate styles. Print out your poem on coloured or textured paper, and the effect is delightful. And this is the one time you can get away with centring your poem, and also breaking the submission rules about coloured papers.

The poem can be placed in a frame, which may be a simple piece of glass clipped to a hardboard back, or a more decorative frame in keeping with the room in which it will be displayed. You can make it into a mini poster. Mount it on card and use poster hangers that can be cut down to size.

You can enhance the appearance of the poem by adding a picture you have sketched or painted, or by making a collage. A tiny spray of dried flowers in the corner of the sheet, diagonally opposite the poem, is particularly attractive. Photographs or brightly coloured postage stamps can be used. Or look at the wide variety of stickers and of embossing stamps available, with every image you can imagine and then some more. Apply the latter with a variety of coloured inks, and the effect can be stunning.

Your crafts shop will be able to provide you with greetings card blanks in a range of colours, with a circular, oval, square or rectangular aperture at the front. A short poem can be slid into place so it is visible through the aperture, and fixed with a touch of glue. You can write your message inside the card - and the whole card can be framed after the event, as described above, or mounted onto the front of a notebook or photograph album.

If the poem is very short, for example a haiku, you could present it in the form of a keyring. You can buy blank perspex keyrings in different sizes, with a separate panel that slots into place when you have put your poem inside.

A slightly longer poem could appear on a small piece of card, perhaps the size of a credit card. The back of the poem is decorated or a second poem is added, and then the work is laminated. (A commercial printer will perform this task for a very small fee). The result is a well-presented poem card to be retained in the wallet or handbag. By printing a name and address on the back of the poem and adding a simple strap through a strategically punched hole, you can produce an original luggage label.

If the shape of the poem allows it, a bookmark can be made in a similar fashion. Square coasters, too, can be done in this way. Or for a more elaborate coaster, your craft shop will supply perspex squares and circles for the purpose, and poems can be clipped into these.

Poems can be painted onto stones, then varnished heavily and displayed either indoors or in the garden. Garden centres provide small stepping stones that are ideally suited to this.

If you are good at needlework, why not present a cross stitch poem sewn onto a background, in the style of the old samplers? It could become a family heirloom, treasured every bit as much as the traditional sampler.

A poem can be mounted on a wooden board such as a bread board, and a collage of items - dried flowers, imitation fruit, miniature flower pots, tiny ornaments, etc. stuck around it. Or try engraving your short poem onto glass, or using special paints to apply it to a mirror.

You can create individual stationery by putting poems in the corner of sheets of paper or onto notelets. Or print your poems on the blank side of plain postcards, allowing the message and address to appear on the other side just as they would on a picture postcard.

These are just a few ideas for having fun with poetry and using craft devices to present it. By trying some and distributing them, you will reach plenty of people who might not think of buying a poetry book - and more importantly, you will be spreading the word that poetry surrounds us today and will stay with us long into the future.

EXERCISES

56 Did you have any eccentric schoolteachers? Recall all you can of their teaching methods, mannerisms, punishments - then get your revenge in a poem.

57 Write a seasonal poem to present in your Christmas cards, or a personal poem for a birthday card. The huge challenge is to try to make it original.

58 Make a list of five fun things to do with poetry or new ways to present the finished piece.

59 Think of a very special time in your life, either a positive or a difficult period. Make notes for eight different poems you could write in connection with it. The links may be close or peripheral. This is an intriguing way to approach poetic autobiography.

60 Write a meta poem - a poem about poetry - showing what poetry means to you. Keep it close at all times. Happy writing!

INDEX

NOTES

Printed in Great Britain
by Amazon